Salvation Through the Gift of Help

Being the tool God intended to help other people his way

By Sandra Joy

Proverbs 16:3
"Commit to the Lord whatever you do, and your plans will succeed.

First published August 2020
Salvation Through the Gift of Help
Copyright Sandra Joy, 2020
Published by Kani Consultants
Lambton, NSW, Australia 2299
Email: sandi.kani@gmail.com

To maintain the privacy of those persons mentioned within this book, names used are not necessarily true. While every attempt has been taken to obtain copy approval throughout, I declare that if any unintentional infringement has occurred, I apologise and will correct it in any reprint.

All rights reserved. Without limiting the rights under copyright reserved above, no part of this publication may be reproduced, stored in or introduced into a database and retrieval system or transmitted in any form or any means (electronic, mechanical, photocopying, recording or otherwise) without the prior written permission of the author.

Original cover illustrations by Estelle Leishman
Typeset by Sandra Boyd
Printed by IngramSpark
ISBN 978-0-909497-19-4 Large Print Paper Back
ISBN 978-0-909497-24-8 Large Print Hard Cover

 A catalogue record for this work is available from the National Library of Australia

Contents

Introduction
Part 1: SALVATION…   11
   Chapter 1: The Help-Save Cycle   13
   Chapter 2: The Purpose of Help   37
   Chapter 3: God is the Example of Help   61
Part 2: Salvation THROUGH…   83
   Chapter 4: In God's Hands   85
   Chapter 5: You're a Tool   109
   Chapter 6: Preparing Yourself for the Job   131
Part 3: Salvation through the GIFT…   157
   Chapter 7: Don't Underestimate the Power of Prayer   159
   Chapter 8: All the Resources   179
   Chapter 9: Desire the Best Gift   199
Part 4: Salvation through the gift of HELP…   221
   Chapter 10: Warning: Bad Help   223
   Chapter 11: The Needees' Needs   247
   Chapter 12: Bless Man & Glorify God   269

Introduction

Why this book?

We live in a very hectic world, with many demands on our time and other resources. Often, our status is based on how busy we are, how productive or rich we appear, or how well-known we are. But are we doing what God intended us to do?

Our calendars may be full of well-meaning acts of service to, and for, other people but do we tend to those duties selflessly? Do these activities have a purpose other than our own gain or reputation? Are others draining the usefulness out of us?

This book shows how we are better able to use the resources God gave us. I hope it helps you to see that he chose you to receive the wonderful gift of helping other people in their daily paths to heaven. No, not by preaching, but by helping.

I aim to show you that, when done the right way, help leads people closer to God and to eternal salvation. In turn, you also develop a closer relationship with God. Everyone wins. Lives are saved when you help people God's way! How exciting is it that we humble helpers get to play a small role in helping people in that process!

Who am I?

More than 30 years ago, God used my Pastor to give me a prophecy, saying that I was to be a *helper* in his ministry. I knew it was from God because the heart of man doesn't want to go out of their way and give up their time and resources for the sake of what other people think they need. Yet, I found myself excited about the prospect of being at God's service.

Unfortunately, being a human, I then spent the next twenty years of my life doing it wrong and being very busy. Now don't misunderstand, along the way I did help a lot of individuals, as well as a lot of committees and businesses. But I truly doubt that I made much eternal difference at all. And that's where I got it wrong, because that is God's main mission after all - eternal salvation for us. Everything that happens on earth is in preparation for eternity with him.

Instead of allowing God to use me with the gift of help, I (yes, *me*) became a helpful human. This 'being helpful' characteristic showed itself throughout my life. In fact, I became known for it, "Good ol' Sandi, she's always so willing to help".

I helped several churches with administration, newsletters, Sunday school, scripture, kids' clubs, women's ministries and youth groups. I helped a Christian School set up its library and canteen; I wrote the newspaper reports and volunteered as a teacher's aide, and was very involved with the P&C (Parents and Citizens Association). I helped a lot of businesses with their administrative, safety and compliance systems.

But there's a distinction between being helpful and helping someone; between helping and operating the Ministry of Help as referred to in 1 Corinthians 12:27-28. The result of God's help is *always* that the recipient comes to know God or comes to know him in a deeper way.

Now, I am not saying that we shouldn't be helpful, what I am saying is that we should live our lives so close to God that he can use us to help when *he* so desires.

My biggest problem was that I became very active doing what I thought were good ideas, filling the needs as I saw them, doing what I thought would be a help to other people. Basically, I was doing what I wanted to do, or my interpretation of what I thought other people wanted me to do. There's no 'I' in God, or in help, but there is in salvation and gift.

Of course, as a young Christian, I didn't realise what was going on. God didn't ask me to "*be helpful.*" He *told me* that *he* was going to *make me "a helper"*. Sadly, it took a long time to discover that these are not the same thing. My type of *helpful* was the human type, and I want to live my life God's way, not mine. I am sure you feel the same way, or you wouldn't be reading this.

It took me twenty years to find out how much time I had wasted doing things *my* way. Please, let me encourage you, don't waste your life. Start doing things God's way. He wrote one plan for each of us and the more time you spend on his plan, the more of your life will be spent doing eternal good.

That's how this book came about, with a longing to live in his will instead of mine. I set to search the scriptures for a job description on what being a helper is meant to look like. Having operated with this gift for over three decades now, I am urged to share my experiences and what I have learned from studying the Biblical interpretation of spiritual help.

When he wants to help someone, he will. If you're not available, he'll use someone else. Why miss out on the blessing of being used by the great God Almighty in His plan for His people? And remember,

God WILL have his way. In the end, how long and how hard the journey is, depends on us.

Throughout this book, unless otherwise stated, I have used the NIV (New International Version) as I find its language easy to understand, and I believe it to be an accurate translation. At other times, I use the KJV (King James Version) to get a better understanding of the original Greek and Hebrew words.

I have also made use of the book, *Strong's Exhaustive Concordance*. This book is more than a dictionary; it gives a link between the definition of the English words to the original Greek and Hebrew sources.

I am currently studying a Bachelor of Arts at the University of Newcastle. I am also a member of the Fellowship of Australian Writers. I recently had a short story published in the Lake Macquarie branch anthology, *Beneath the Surface*, and won third place in the Odyssey House Short Story Competition 2019.

Believe it or not, at birth I was given the name Sandra Joy (surname irrelevant). Sandra means Helper and Joy means Happy. So call me the "Happy Helper". Looking back, I can see just how prophetic my parents were in naming me that. Happy reading.

Application

When God created the world, he didn't then walk away and forget about it. Likewise, it is not in our best interests to learn something and then walk away and forget about it. Our lives are an ongoing lifestyle full of change and commitments, so when God instructed us to continue to learn and to grow, we need to apply what we learn along the way.

At the end of each of God's creation days, he reflected on what he had done, and he saw that it was good. On the seventh day, he rested - but I am sure he didn't ignore or neglect his works. I think he would have enjoyed the fruits of his labour. I want you to keep living in what you are doing, **live within the changes you have made!**

To live in those changes, and so this doesn't become just another one of those books you read and shelve (yes, we've all done it) I have added a few questions at the end of each chapter. I hope these help you to think about, and apply, what you have read.

Obviously, whether or not you do these application questions is up to you. You may simply want to understand the gift of help and may not want to apply it to your life. If this is you, then just skip over those pages. But, if you are keen to serve God and have a calling in this area, I encourage you to dig deeper and answer them.

Another method is to read this with a small Bible study group and share your weekly progress with others. God sees what you do anyway, and you are accountable only to him in this journey, but it is very beneficial to have human eyes watching, and other people to share with and learn from.

This book is also relevant for those who may not go to church but want to develop and maintain a close relationship with God.

Whichever way you choose to read this book, I hope it stretches you and makes you excited about being a part of God's workings in this world we live in. Helping others to come to know God or to come into a deeper relationship with him is definitely worth a little inconvenience!

Acknowledgements:

There are so many people to thank, but I must firstly thank God himself for his perseverance and patience with me through the journey of this project.

Thank you to my family who constantly encouraged me to follow this through to the end. To my children for being the wonderful, strong and incredible people you are. Even if you weren't mine, I'd choose each of you. To Rob, for always seeing the positive and being the family rock. To Jess, for never giving up on yourself, and for the hours of background work. To Kelly, for teaching me about 'adulting' and for always being there no matter the distance between us. To Julie, for your endless prayers and encouragement. To Ron, for putting up with the crazy hours and supporting me no matter what obsession I take.

Thank you to those who have mentions in this book, for being so open to having your personal stories shared with strangers. This book is about people and for people, and your willingness to help is much appreciated. To my critique team who read, suggested, discussed and commented … hour after hour, page after page. Mr Trubl, you are amazing. To Estelle, who patiently took my unclear ideas and creatively produced the beautiful cover and associated merchandise.

Thanks to all those who have responded to the call of God to help other people. For the readers who want to know God better and be at his service to help other people, may you continue to bless man and glorify God with your life.

Love to all of you in one of the Ministries of Christ,

Sandra Joy

Part 1: SALVATION …

Salvation comes in many forms. Some people need to be saved from an abusive partner. Others need to be saved from a flood. Some from the grips of alcohol.

The one salvation that all humans need is salvation from their sins, and we know that Jesus is the answer for that. For Christians, beliefs and salvation go hand in hand. They are fundamental principles. Simply, you believe in God and know with confidence that he offers salvation for those who believe in him.

Now, if you have the ministry of being a pastor, or the gift of witnessing then you are already helping in that salvation process. For those who don't, I'd like you to see that it is not necessary to be a pastor or a missionary, or to have the 'gift of the gab' to be able to reach people. You just need to help them.

Without detracting from God's miraculous powers and intervention, I'd also like you to consider salvation as a process rather than a one-step miracle. As we go through this book, we will look at this process as a cycle, the cycle of helping people that leads to salvation, the Help-Save Cycle. In part one, I will challenge you to look at your goals as we consider the purpose of helping others and view God as the ultimate example of help.

SALVATION...

Chapter 1: The Help-Save Cycle

Helping someone is usually considered a linear task - they have a problem, you provide the solution, end of problem. Unfortunately, life is rarely that straightforward or simple.

God has asked us to be aware of the problems around us and, rather than taking them at face value or thinking that we are the answer, to trust God.

Many ways of thinking

I once heard someone say that "it takes 20 years to become an overnight success". And, while it is not always that precise, the message is true - nothing happens instantly.

You may disagree. A car accident is instant, so is an incoming phone call. These actions appear to you instantly, but take a moment to think about them. Look at every step and decision that occurred previously to make them happen in the manner, location and time that they did. Were they really instantaneous?

Like childbirth or death, everything has a process. I started writing this book more than two decades ago and I'm working on another one that is the culmination of 52 years of experience.

What has all this got to do with helping people?

People don't instantly get into situations where they require help. Nor does their rescue happen that quickly. There is a process, a sequence of events, to getting in - and out of - trouble.

When someone finds themselves *suddenly* in trouble, you can guarantee that there were steps that brought them to that exact point in time. Many other factors and people played a role in that journey. The trouble had a prelude, a struggle, and it has a solution. It also has a maintenance or preventative strategy to avoid repetition (it's there, whether or not it's followed).

Fortunately, saving people from their situation is part of a cycle that allows us to intervene in that sequence of events. It is not a straight line or a checklist. You do not simply see a need, wave a wand, follow a few generic steps and the problem is solved forever. If that were the case, most mothers would use this for domestic duties so they didn't have to make the bed every day and clean up constantly.

Life is not an instant-fix process. Thankfully, your part in solving most problems is flexible. You simply need to be willing to be a part of the cycle of help.

Your willingness to be a helper for God does not fit neatly into the methods used by many churches today. Often, churches will assign roles based on the traditional lists found in the Bible.

Romans 12:6 tells us that we have different gifts - prophesy, serving, teaching, encouraging, giving, leadership, and mercy.

Then 1 Corinthians 12:8-11 shares the gifts that the Holy Spirit gives - wisdom, knowledge, faith, healing, miraculous powers, prophecy, distinguishing spirits, speaking in tongues, and interpreting tongues.

Unfortunately, some churches box people into these roles and even judge people according to the *gifts* they possess. Do you think God truly intended to limit people in that way? Doesn't the Bible teach us that all parts work together? And, if they are *gifts*, then how can we be judged for what someone (God) gives to us? What's more, the focus should be on ensuring others are saved, not what people can, or can't, do.

Today's English speakers apply the term 'saved' to a complex range of problems. Let's quickly look at salvation and the many uses of that word. According to the Concise Oxford Dictionary, the noun 'salvation' has two meanings:

1. The act of saving or being saved; preservation from loss, calamity etc;
2. Deliverance from sin and its consequences and admission to heaven, brought about by Christ;

Using the second definition, salvation can come in the form of:

- spiritual - your soul can be saved when you commit your life to Jesus and know you are going to heaven when you die.

At this point, you may think I want you to be a religious zealot and only focus on the spiritual form of saving others. That's definitely not what I want. All scenarios where people find themselves in need of saving are opportunities to use the tool of help.

Using the first definition, salvation can come in many forms:

- physical - your life is saved from a rip in the ocean, a burning building or the attack of a wild animal;
- mental - your sanity, or stress levels, can be saved when an when an assistant takes some of the work from you; when you get a much-needed holiday, or a problem is solved;
- emotional - a friend can save you from a breakdown by lending a shoulder or an ear; a psychologist may save you from your depressed state by providing counselling; a comedy or good news story may help put things in perspective when life seems overwhelming or unfair;
- financial - a bank may save you from bankruptcy when they extend your loan; your parents may save you from being evicted by paying your rent or buying your groceries; or a financial adviser may help you by teaching you how to budget and save.

The thing these examples all have in common is that, at some point, to be saved from the situation requires some type of **help**. I dare say, to be saved from *any* situation requires help. Otherwise you would stay exactly where you are, with nothing changing.

Once you start thinking about situations where people require help, open your mind to the variables made possible by the number of people and circumstances in everyday life. Dealing with this number of issues is only possible because of the God that we know and love, as only he knows every individual's situation personally, and tends to every need individually.

If I am assuming that you are a Christian, then you have probably known other people who have come to know the Lord. Maybe you played a role in someone's conversion, or maybe in many. Well done! Please keep up the great work; but don't stop reading yet though.

Over the years, I have heard countless testimonies of Christians about their salvation, including:
- "It took years to convince me"
- "I grew up in a Christian home, but walked away before making a personal decision"
- "I was studying to disprove the Bible when I became a believer"
- "God spoke to me and I suddenly knew he was real"
- "My grandmother prayed for me every day and one day it worked"
- "I wanted what they had so I went to church one day"
- "I fought it for so long, believing I wasn't good enough, then ..."

The point is, not one of those salvations was a solo act. Don't ever think that we can save ourselves. Our passport to heaven includes the work of God the Father, Jesus, the Holy Spirit, the person being converted and, in addition to this, God usually uses at least one other person to pray, teach or help that person - way before the decision is made by the human.

Though the destination is the same, the road to salvation is always unique. That's one of the reasons why you hear testimonies in most charismatic churches. They acknowledge that the moment of salvation, and the journey to that point, are as individual as the person involved.

It is important to realise that no two people have the same story. Every person's story is distinct. While a multitude of people can go through the same experience, everyone goes through it with different attitudes and abilities which stem from the experiences they have already encountered. The combination of their individual past makes them unique, even though they may currently be in the same position that others are in. (We will discuss later how this position then becomes a source available for others to learn from). If everyone's story was identical, it would lose its meaning and impact. If every journey was the same, why bother travelling? In fact, why live at all if every life was the same?

There are numerous ways of coming to the conscious realisation that we need to believe in God, to get into relation with him, and gain entry to heaven. You and I have a role to play in helping other people along that road, not always leading them to the end, but helping them at various stages.

As you will see, there are many problems with many solutions. The one bank does not loan to every client in the world. The one medical professional does not treat every illness and injury, nor are they treated in the same way. God uses the tools most suitable and accessible at the time. Our role is only a small part in the process of salvation, but each stage is as important as the other in a person seeing eternal salvation.

Neither salvation nor helping someone is an action that occurs instantly. The process of getting to the point of needing to be saved, then acknowledging it, requires a change of heart and mind. And the help is not immediate. The best type of help needs to be determined, sourced and approached. They need to be ready to accept the mission. Then the change needs to be implemented.

Neither salvation nor daily struggles have a quick-fix one-step solution. There are a lot of ways of thinking about helping others, about people's needs and the way we help, but one thing is for sure, when we do, we need to trust God.

Key Points:
- Getting to the position of needing help doesn't happen instantly;
- Helping someone in need is not the end of the problem;
- The term 'saved' is relevant to every aspect of life;
- Only God knows every situation intimately;
- Helping is never a solo act.

Trust God

In Mark 5:36, when asked about a dead girl, Jesus answered, "Don't be afraid; just believe." If that was his response to bringing a dead daughter back to life, how much simpler is it for him to give us the tools to help his people.

In Philippians chapter 4, Paul expressed his gratitude for the Philippians' concern for him. He then talks about his learned ability to be content in every situation. In verse 13 he states simply that, "I can do everything through him who gives me strength."

Have you been confronted with an opportunity to help, but thought the task too menial or too hard, or that you just couldn't do it? Let's see how important God thinks helping is. "In Joppa there was a disciple named Tabitha who was always doing good and *helping* the poor ... she became sick and died...Peter got down on his knees and prayed...she opened her eyes." (Acts 9:36-40)

She opened her eyes! *This* is how important helping is to God. He just cannot bear to lose one of His helpers. I am not saying helpers are more important than anyone else. I am not saying that God will resurrect every helper who dies. I am saying that this is the only mention of her in the Bible, and her resurrection story would have worked even without mentioning that she was a helper, so it has to be important.

Just like Peter, we have access to these miraculous powers because the Holy Spirit lives within us too. If God wanted to use us to raise people from the dead, who are we to stand in His way of doing just that!

In Psalm 146:3 we are instructed not to trust man for salvation; we need to trust God for that. Equally, we are not to trust man for help, we need to trust God for that too. The KJV says, "Put not your trust in princes, nor in the son of man, in whom there is no *help*." The same verse in the NIV says, "Do not put your trust in princes, in mortal men, who cannot *save*."

Look at the final phrases in each of these translations: "no help" and "cannot save". These translations, written by religious and literary experts, gives us a hint at what helping is all about - salvation. The words *help* and *save* are interchangeable, as are their meanings.

Psalm 37:40 says "And the Lord shall help them, and deliver them: He shall deliver them from the wicked, and save them, because they trust in Him." This verse summarises the entire message of this Psalm. There will always be evildoers, but put your trust in God and he WILL deliver you from them. The previous verse states, "the salvation of the righteous is of the Lord".

Notice that he does not promise to miraculously remove the problem. He promises to HELP them in the problem and deliver them out of it – to make sure they survive through to the end. Often, Christians expect God to answer their prayers of help by removing the mountain, or sending a cheque for a million dollars out of nowhere. People will pray when they play the pokies or buy a lotto ticket. There's a problem there. God wants us to be totally reliant on him, He does not want us to gamble and 'take our chances'. He wants 100% trust in him.

One of the things that makes God different from us is that he is capable of helping everyone. Have you ever stopped to consider how many people need help at any one time? Let's do some maths.

According to trending ads and the internet, adults make about 35,000 remotely conscious decisions each day. That's a lot of opportunities for 'sliding door' moments where our actions have an effect on ourselves and other people. I personally found that number ridiculous, but consider just a few: do I want a coffee, what type; will I change lanes in front of that car; black or blue jeans, smile or not … The moments quickly add up.

According to Worldometer on 19 March 2020, the world currently holds 7,771,790,870 people. Let's round that up to 7.8 billion. It also states that the average life expectancy is 73.2 years. Time to calculate.

Taking the average, one person living to 73.2 years at 365.25 days in a year (allowing for leap years) means that one person lives for 26,736.3 days. We know that each day contains 24 hours each with 60 minutes, each with 60 seconds. So, one day is made up of 86,400 seconds. Wow!

So, the average person lives for 26,736.3 x 86,400 seconds. This is a staggering 2,310,016,320 seconds in the average lifetime. Just for argument's sake, if we consider a 'moment' in time to be a second, the average person has 2,310,016,320 moments in their life. That's huge!

And that's only *one* person. One person who is alive at this point in history. And there are currently 7,771,790,870 alive. Can we possibly calculate the number of moments in the lifetimes of each human that is alive in this very moment?

How many humans do you think have lived on this earth? How many more are yet to be born? How many human beings will this world hold in its life? I can't even contemplate that number. God can.

What I do know is, by looking at life and time in this method, there is a lot happening. At any given second there is an unfathomable number of problems, issues, mistakes, hurts, accidents, careless behaviours, and uneducated or selfish decisions being experienced by individuals.

If you then consider that somewhere in the process, these involve more than one person, the number becomes colossal. Then add global events like war, poverty, pandemic or drought and the effects on individuals become even more mind-blowing. Life now seems insurmountable, but not to God.

Consider one person who is in debt. Maybe you have been there yourself. That person has a lot to contend with and needs to prioritise where their money goes. One bill they may struggle to pay is rent. Who is affected if they don't pay their rent? The real estate agent - whose business could close, and staff would be out of work if all their tenants fell into debt. The owner of the house - who has at least one mortgage to pay, and could find themselves and their family struggling, or even homeless.

Every action has a reactive consequence and, as we saw above, there are a *lot* of actions happening simultaneously! And God is looking at, and dealing with, all of them. How? Have you heard the saying, "God couldn't be everywhere, that's why he created mothers?" In a flippant way, there is some truth in that. We know that God is everywhere, and that he is capable of working miracles, but he chooses methods that involve us humans, and by doing so, everyone benefits.

- The person in **need** benefits from being open and, admitting they are fallible, and identifying what they need to improve their situation;
- The selected **tool** benefits from being chosen by God for his purpose, the lessons learned, the satisfaction felt, and the growth that comes from putting others first;
- The person in need benefits from the **help** given, whether it's love or assistance;
- God benefits from the glory and **praise** that is, rightfully, given Him;
- The non-Christian benefits when they accept Christ's offered **salvation** and the Christian benefits by an enhanced relationship with God;

- Now in relation with God, they benefit from the confidence of being able to call on him more easily when in **need** ... and the cycle continues.

That flat line is taking a curve - one need is solved, and another is seen. There is no end. Our role isn't to solve the world's problems. Our role is to trust in God and be available when he asks for us. To be available, we need to know him.

Key Points:
- The words 'help' and 'save' are interchangeable;
- The key to helping is knowing what God wants for that person in that situation;
- God doesn't promise an easy life, he promises opportunities to learn and grow;
- Don't stand in the way of God's big plans;
- No matter how much is required, God is more than capable.

Salvation comes through helping others

The world is full of devastation and destruction. Among this, two common misconceptions are often heard: "If God loved us then he would fix everything;" and, "If God loved us, why does he allow bad things like earthquakes?"

I challenge these with a simple parental perspective. "If mum loved me then she would let me do anything I wanted;" and, "If dad loved me then he would never discipline me."

Being loved does not mean getting everything you want. Being loved does not mean you will have a perfect life.

God could 'magically' fix everything upon demand, but there are a lot of reasons for not solving certain issues at certain times. This doesn't mean God can't, it just means he is loving and wise enough not to do it in the method and timing that *we* think he should. Remember, how many moments or issues there are at any time - God has a much better perspective on our lives than we do.

There is no point in giving money to an addict, because of the risk that they will use that cash to purchase whatever fix they require at the time – alcohol, drugs, gambling, porn or other. You may be better giving cash to the partner of an alcoholic who can put it towards food or rent. God knows these intricacies about us and the other people in our paths.

How do you know how to respond to the request? By knowing the truth in the circumstances. Sometimes that means getting to know the person, other times that means trusting for God's guidance and direction in a situation. Other times it involves using common sense or wisdom.

We live in this world among the suffering, but God doesn't expect us to know all the details, just be willing to play our part. The ultimate result of helping is salvation and, in that process, bringing people closer in their relationship with God, including you.

There is a model that has been around for a long time and has been expanded on by therapists and religious persons alike. The Belief-Expectation Cycle simply says that:
- Changing your beliefs changes your expectations;
- Changing your expectations changes your attitude;
- Changing your attitude changes your behaviour;
- Changing your behaviour changes your life.

This model is used to encourage good beliefs, but also applies to bad. It suggests that good beliefs result in a good life and bad beliefs result in a bad life. While it is referred to as a cycle, it actually portrays a linear process with a clear beginning and ending. While I agree with the steps, I don't want you to stop at the end.

Instead, I am going to adopt this model throughout this book, and apply it to another: the Help-Save Cycle.

- In part 1, I hope to help you change your **beliefs** to see that helping has an eternal purpose, and to see the role that helping plays in salvation. It is part of a much bigger plan than what is immediately in front of you.
- In part 2, I hope to help you change your **expectations** in helping you to allow God to work **through** you, rather than travelling this journey separately.
- In part 3, I hope to help you change your **attitude** to see this as **the gift** God has chosen to give you. That he chose *you* as the recipient of this gift.
- In part 4, I hope to help you change your **behaviour** and show you some ways to put into practice the work **of help.**

Have you noticed that helping others has the potential to open the heart of both the giver and the receiver?

By trusting God, I am reminded that this world is not just about me and what I want. Then, being willing to help humbly reminds me that God is in control and we are merely tools in his hands. The world does not revolve around me.

Seeing God work through us mere mortals is one of the most exhilarating feelings. We become excited when we see God's work, which brings us closer to him and makes us more eager to help him next time he asks. It's a bit like helping a grateful relative (or friend, colleague or neighbour) as opposed to a selfish one. Helping the grateful one results in lunch and drinks, fun and a feeling of appreciation, and a willingness to be there the next time they ask. As humans, however, helping the selfish person can leave us feeling used and frustrated, our time being wasted, and has us running with excuses next time.

Can you see how we also change from helping others? We become closer to God when we obey his directions and commands. Not only can helping people lead to their salvation but my salvation is affected too. Helping others helps to confirm my salvation through deepening my relationship with God. Here are some of the ways:

- Drawing on this gift draws me closer to God;
- Obeying and trusting him deepens our relationship;
- Longing to help others humbly reminds me of the correct priorities in life;
- Crown jewels are on promise;
- It reminds me that I live *in* this world, but I am not *of* it.

God reveals his love and plans to us slowly and in the manner we individually relate. In 1 Samuel chapters 9-10 we see God giving Saul signs. He gives these signs through others who are so close to God that they can be used as tools.

God's tools can do a range of tasks, whether passing on a message like Samuel, or giving a stranger a book.

We may never know or understand the relevance of the sign to the recipient and, more importantly, we don't need to. That's between them and God. The wonder of God is that they may not even know what sign they need. They may ask for something completely different, or not even ask at all.

We may not be the ones to see the results, but by planting seeds, we are opening the hearts and minds of others. One day, they will reach out to God with longing and gratitude. But the result *is* salvation, new or deepened! By Samuel knowing God, he became obedient to him. Through his obedience, God was able to use him as a tool. In his role as a tool for God he *simply* passed on a message from God (1 Sam 9:27). The result is seen a little later in chapter 10 verse 6 with Saul. "The Spirit of the Lord will come upon you in power, and you will prophesy with them; and you will be changed into a different person."

Then in 10:7 we read, "Once these signs are fulfilled, do whatever your hand finds to do, for God is with you." Wow. Samuel was so close to God that he would be doing only God's will and God would use all of these works. I want to live like Samuel. Then I would never waste any more time.

Messages from the Bible are as relevant today as they were then. Let's learn from the lessons of these two men. Let's read the signs and know God better. After all, out of SAmUeL came SAUL and me.

Two problems exist with the Belief-Expectation Cycle. Firstly, it is a perfectionist view, expecting everything to end up perfect and in no further need of change. Secondly, since it is a linear plan, it's not a cycle, and this removes all hope once you reach the end of it. I am going to introduce you to a cycle that allows for the imperfections of man, the Help-Save Cycle.

Key Points:
- God loves us enough to help us in the best way;
- Salvation is a process that we have a role in;
- Helping others strengthens our relationship with God;
- God gives signs that we don't need to understand;
- Helping isn't just about salvation for non-Christians.

The Help-Save Cycle

Many housewives jokingly complain to each other, "If only the house would stay clean" or "I make the bed and they sleep in it again." Wouldn't it be nice if we could do things just once? Shop and the fridge stays stocked. Clean and the house stays clean. Instruct and they adhere to that rule in every instance. This is only a fantasy of course and, in reality, what would we learn from living like that?

The cycle of help is just that, a cycle. In a perfect world it would be a straight line - once the problem was fixed, we would acknowledge our maker and stay in close relation with him. Unfortunately, it is a continual cycle, because even as Christians, we have needs. I find that sad as it reminds me just how many times we humans fall away from our relationship with God and from living the life that He intended for us. But then I am excited that it is a cycle because I am reminded of his patience and love and that he is *always* there to meet us where we're at and do whatever is necessary to bring us back.

Because God loves all people, the cycle of salvation applies to both Christians and non-Christians. Helping doesn't just result in salvation for non-Christians. In fact, that's a very narrow-sighted view, which would also lead to an unhealthy hierarchy. This then leads to thinking like, "I am better than them; that's why I must help unfortunate non-believers, so those poor people can get to heaven." This thinking is opposite to the attitude of salvation and helping we are supposed to have!

I see the book of 1 Samuel as a comparison of today's world. Struggles for, and with, leadership; on and off again relationship with sin and God; greed and war; God's patience and wrath. And between it all, his strong desire and innate unmatchable ability to help.

The Help-Save Cycle Explained

The Concise Oxford Dictionary defines the word needy as: "Poor, destitute".

I should explain that, when I use the word 'needy', I am not referring to the common definition of one who is disadvantaged and deprived. Rather, come with me as I invent a new pair of words. Think of words like employer and employee, payer and payee, trainer and trainee. A person who is the object of the verb, to whom an action is done. So, I have 'done a Shakespeare' and created my own words. In this book, one who provides help is a helper. Therefore, one who is helped is a helpee (rhymes with trainee, not Kelpie). Using the same grammatical rules, one who provides for a need is a needer. So, one who is subject to, or in need, is a needee. These people, in God's eyes, are not necessarily destitute, poor or insecure. A person's needs usually go way beyond what other people see.

Need: The needee cry out for help. Christians know they can call God directly, but his offer to help does not apply only to those who already know him. If your child needed help, you would oblige without question. If your child's school friend needed help, you would also make yourself available. How much more is God willing to help any member of the human race. After all, he did make every one of us. The reality is that non-Christians, like many believers, will call out to other sources first. Alternatively, they may simply think about what they need for their current situation, without prayerfully discussing it with God. But God knows the heart of every man and meets us where we are at. So, whether or not us humans ask God for help, he knows what we need. He can identify the needs of every person.

Tool: God selects the right tool for every situation. Being omnipresent (everywhere) and omnipotent (all-knowing), he knows exactly what each person needs at any given time. He is not going to send a vegetable peeler to paint a wall. And he has the world's resources at his fingertips ready to aide those in need: a miraculous storm, an extra set of hands, or money. Sometimes, we question his methods, just as children question their parents, but we should never doubt his motivation.

Help: God, through his chosen helper / tool, provides the help that is required. This may be teaching, food, a delay in the due date for a bill, or a prayer. Regardless of the type of need, there will be an action.

Praise: The needee praise God. Christians acknowledge God's hand in the situation and give him the thanks, praise that is rightfully his. Non-Christians may hear the Christian helper praising God or realise that they have been listening to the promptings of the Holy Spirit. In turn, they will praise God - maybe not instantly or verbally, but the seed is planted.

Salvation: By acknowledging the help, non-Christians accept salvation and Christians praise and / or repent, getting closer to God. New Christians are not instantly made perfect. They are more like babies or foreigners to a new land - in need of help to develop and grow in their new environment.

As I explained earlier, this is a cycle, not a straight line. Life doesn't suddenly become perfect once a person accepts Christ and becomes saved. We still need help.

The cycle continues unceasingly. Using the example of a person in a rip, once that issue has been resolved, the experience is not over. The emergency has passed. The situation has passed. The experience lives on in that person's life. It may cause them to improve their swimming strength. It may cause Post Traumatic Stress Disorder (PTSD). They may use their knowledge to help other people caught in rips. They may use it to teach other people how to get out of them, or how to identify and avoid them. They may use the experience to acknowledge how fragile life is and how grateful they are to God for saving their life. They may, in their next crisis, turn directly to God in prayer and thanks. They may learn that they can depend on God, and develop a relationship with him, leading to their eternal salvation.

And, if they stop thinking about it, I guarantee it's not the last time they have a need. Our journey through life, and helping others through theirs, is nothing short of a miraculous process.

The time, the path and the experiences along the way, vary between every single human being. Our experiences are not to be wasted. Our experiences give us the inside knowledge and skills to relate to others in similar circumstances, making us tools in God's hands.

Are you willing to use your experiences to help lead others to Christ and eternal salvation?

Are you willing to use your own experiences to develop a closer relationship with God, compounding your salvation?

Are you willing to give God the glory for the experiences you, and others, go through, acknowledging his strength and love and purpose for all?

Are you willing to find out what God has in plan for your life and the true purpose of helping others?

Before we go any further, I want you to understand that, while helping is a tool for salvation, not everyone will accept the salvation offered to them. Helping provides the opportunity, a mechanism, but sadly, does not always lead to salvation. The kindergarten teacher may have an enormous influence on the lives of those five-year-olds, but he or she is not responsible if that child drops out of school in year 9. The teacher has done their bit to enable them to travel on a path to successfully complete their education to year 12 and beyond. They cannot be held accountable for the consequences and decisions that influenced their students later in life.

Likewise, you can do your bit in helping others, but their salvation decision is not your responsibility.

Key Points:
- The cycle reminds us of God's love and patience;
- Need - Tool - Help - Praise - Salvation - Repeat;
- Helping others through their life's journey is a miraculous process;
- Our experiences make us useful tools in God's hands;
- Not accepting the offer is their choice, not your failure.

Application for Chapter 1: The Help-Save Cycle

1. Name at least 3 people involved in your eternal salvation and what role they each played?

   _____

   _____

   _____

2. Where are you currently on the cycle of help? (You may select more than one)
   - ☐ I have a need
   - ☐ I am a tool available for use
   - ☐ God is using me to help someone
   - ☐ I am praising God for a recent solution
   - ☐ My salvation is new and / or growing

3. Think of someone you know who has a situation where they need help. What is, or was, your initial response to this realisation?

   _____

   _____

   _____

4. Recall a time when you helped someone with a problem. What was the need? What did you do to help? What was the result? Describe the feelings you had afterwards. What did / could you say to God after this event?

_____

_____

_____

5. Select one Bible reference mentioned in this chapter. Write it out on another piece of paper and put it on your fridge. Memorise it this week. Now, write it here in your own words.

_____

_____

_____

6. Based on what you have read so far, write down an area that you have seen God at work in your life.

_____

_____

_____

7. Spend some time talking to God about the things you have recorded in the questions above.

SALVATION...

Chapter 2: The Purpose of Help

God made us to help others, not to be self-centred, greedy or lazy. Right from the beginning, God created people to be helpers. He made Eve as a helper for Adam, and he gave Adam the responsibility of helping the environment by caring for it. In both cases, love and help work simultaneously.

God's purpose was not selfish. It was always his intention for us to spend time with him - in the Garden of Eden, beyond that into the rest of the world, and in Heaven. Still today, helping is an opportunity to tell others about God, his love for us, and Christ's offer of salvation. It is an opportunity to tell others that God wants to help them so much more than we mere humans can.

Your Goal or God's?

Accepting that helping is God's desire, not ours, will help us see our role in it. Isaiah 35:3-5 shows us the process of helping his way. In his order: first we help others; then we witness; and then God helps.

"*Strengthen the feeble* hands ... ; *say to those* with fearful hearts, "Be strong ... *he* [God] *will come to save you*," *Then* will ...". Helping is not a random exercise, it has purpose.

In 1 Samuel 12:22 we are told, "For the sake of his great name the Lord will not reject his people." We sin, and, if we repent, he forgives us. Not because we are any great individual, not because we are worthy, but because he has a much bigger plan. He wants us in relationship with him, and he wants to use our failings and shortfalls to develop that relationship.

While he doesn't promise to give us a perfect life, he does try to make our lives easier for us along the way. We just need to understand that his idea of what is good for us is often quite different from the human version. To some, an *easy* life means lots of money, lots of assets and lots of holidays. Whereas, to God, none of that is important. His idea of making our lives easy is not even based on taking away the struggle, but more about making sense of it. It is often through the suffering that we grow and draw closer to him.

How often do you revise how you spend your assets? You have money. How should you best spend it? You *are* going to spend it. So, what is the best way? What about your car or caravan, are you generous with them?

What about your time and other resources? What about your thoughts? How should that time be best spent? After all, you *are* going to spend it. You are going to use every moment of your life, expel every breath, until you die - so what will you do with it all?

Think about your education, both formal and informal. You are going to learn a lot of things in your life, whether they are useless or useful, expensive or cheap.

The point here is that we all have valuable assets at our fingertips. Assets that God has given and can, at any time, add to or take away. We need to make the conscious choice to best use our assets in line with his purpose. This is the first step to determining whether we live our lives under God's goals or our own. Don't get me wrong; I am not suggesting you give everything away, run to the hills and become a monk! Quite the opposite.

In fact, I am not advocating giving up work, money, activities or relationships at all. I am simply asking you to address your motivation. If you are tempted, or need more clarity on this, I strongly recommend reading the book, *Called to Create*.

In it (on page 181), Jordan Raynor shares the difference between people whose motive for preaching the gospel is helping and winning souls, and those whose motive is selfish gain. I highly recommend this book.

Continue to help your partner, kids, your church, and your community - God wants that - but to best help, we need to arm ourselves with useful tools. Just as you make selections and decisions that better your career or family, make them to better fulfil God's purpose for you and your relationship with him.

Have you ever noticed the skills in a pastor's family? Is it a coincidence that most Christian ministers and their families have a range of skills including preaching, teaching, childcare, housekeeping, and music? Sometimes our arsenal of helpful tools is obvious; sometimes it isn't. In 1 Samuel 16:14-23 we see that David was a worker with a hobby. He was then anointed and called to use his skills to help Saul. David was chosen to serve because of his ability to play the harp, not because anyone thought he would later kill that giant, Goliath.

How can God use your skills for bigger things? Are your motives ready for his service? If a friend was moving to a new house and asked for your help, would you:

A. Ask them (or yourself) how you benefit from this;

B. Say no without thinking;

C. Say yes without thinking; or

D. Trust in the fact that you had asked God that morning to guide your day, and so rest comfortably in your decision - whatever that may be. Then ask God to best use you in that situation.

Being available to be a helper means being willing *not* to be in control of your life. It is a good thing to be organised and know what you have in mind to do each day, but many theorists will also tell you to be flexible. As busy and as organised as I like to be, I support that concept. Having plans ensures that the important things get done, and things are done more efficiently. However, when working for God, as our plans don't always match up with his, our days can be chaotic.

Can you relate to this type of day: I plan to work on my novel all day. What happens is: mum comes to visit, I have to pick up a sick kid from school, I need to go to the shop, and then it's time to cook tea, so I end my day in frustration. Then I realise that I didn't best utilise this day by starting with: "God, what's *your* plan for me today?"

The time will come when we need to accept that God's way is better than ours. Psalm 60:11 has been translated differently, but are more powerful when we look at them together.

The KJV says: "Give us help from trouble: for *vain is the help of man*."

The NIV says: "Give us aid against the enemy, for *the help of man is worthless*."

What strong words, the help of man is *vain* and *worthless*. Hallelujah!!! Once we realise this, we will let God take over and things will go much better for everyone!

Neil T. Anderson makes a lot of valid points in his book *Renewing Your Mind*. I have extracted a few from one section: "A godly goal is any specific orientation that reflects God's purpose for our lives and that is not dependent on people or circumstances beyond our right or ability to control.... The only person who can keep me from reaching that goal is me!... A godly desire is any specific result that depends on the cooperation of other people, the success of events, or favourable circumstances that we have no right or ability to control." (Anderson 70)

So, looking at Neil's book in short, a godly goal:
- reflects God's purpose for me;
- is not dependent on anyone or anything else; and
- acknowledges that the only person who can keep me from reaching it is ME.

What is the best goal for your life? As much as you organise your life, you may never know. But rest assured in that old saying, "God is more interested in your life than you are."

Why don't you take a moment to reflect on some of your goals? What purpose are they serving? Whose purpose are they serving, yours or God's? In this section, I have recommended several great resources to help you develop and grow. Their details can be found in the back of this book if you would like to take some time now to order any through a bookstore or library. (I have no affiliations with any of them, I just value you). Then please return for chapter 3.

Key Points:
- We grow through suffering;
- Consciously decide how to use your assets of time, education, money;
- David was chosen to play a harp, not to kill a giant;
- The help of man is vain and worthless;
- Whose purpose are your goals serving?

We don't need to see the outcome

Seeing the result is not the purpose of helping someone. In fact, we may never know the outcome of the work we do - and that's as it should be. In saying that, I do love it when God chooses to share the results of his work with us.

I am reminded of a situation where God used me to reunite a mother and son. Elizabeth and her son, Keith, had become estranged in recent months, both caught up in their own separate worlds.

Keith rang me one night, and the two of us spoke at length about all the changes happening in his life and he touched on the awkward relationship with his parents. The conversation lasted a full 40 minutes. A lot of words are spoken in that length of time, but there was one sentence that jumped out to me. It was as if my internal volume went up only over those words. He hadn't emphasised it. It wasn't the main topic. The Holy Spirit was highlighting it in my mind.

Keith said to me, "Sometimes, I just wanna talk to my mum, ya know."

And I did know. I knew what he meant. I had experienced distance from my own children at different times, but this wasn't just empathy. These words wouldn't let go. Over the next 12 hours they kept playing in my mind. I heard them on repeat, I felt them deeply and I pondered with the idea of telling his mum.

This wasn't gossip; it wasn't even something I wanted to do. I didn't think it was my place to get involved, and I knew I would be torn emotionally if I were to hear both versions. Besides, I had no solutions to their issues and all logic said to maintain the confidence of the conversation with Keith. Yet this was something that I was compelled to do. So, I told his mum about the conversation and, putting it in context, I repeated his son's comment, "Sometimes, I just wanna talk to my mum, ya know."

She cried.

She then told me something I had no possible way of knowing. Only the night before (probably when I was on the phone to Keith) she had been worrying that she was going to lose contact with her son for good. Now she knew that this was God's perfect timing and *she* had to act, and *now*.

Do you remember the Help-Save Cycle? This was one example of God hearing the need. And I was not only relieved, but blessed, to be a part of it. Despite us not needing to know the background details or the outcome, it is always comforting when God confirms your actions are indeed His.

The story gets even better.

Elizabeth took the step of faith and made contact. She arranged to go and see her son that Saturday. They both had a lovely time together – rare for them not to come away angry at, or hurt by, the other. To confirm, Keith sent his mum an email that night thanking her for the lovely day they had.

And then, as if that wasn't enough, they had another day together on the Sunday! Two days in a row and not sick of each other.

And *still* the story doesn't end. I visited Keith a week later and mentioned that his mum had told me about the lovely time they had together.

His reply was this: "I thought to myself, Sandi has talked to mum. Sandi, thank you!"

My reply: "It was a God thing."

He said: "I know, like…." And he told me about another miracle.

When God's purpose is done, the result is that someone receives some type of blessing and God gets the glory for it. In short, and you will hear me use this phrase a lot: *bless man and glorify God!*

If you don't already, I strongly recommend you take advantage of modern technology and download a daily Bible verse app. I use *YouVersion* Bible app and have the settings to receive the daily *Verse of the Day*. I also receive a daily email verse and message from "Alive to God".

Please don't treat these like horoscope readings. They are not your 'lucky message or prediction for your day'. Look at them as reminders, written by men and women who have spent a lot of time studying the word of God. They send the same verse to thousands of people, so they are not specifically written for you on that day, but God can use them and will often *highlight* something to you. Just like those words of Keith's spoke to me. The Bible is the *living* word and the Holy Spirit lives *within* you – unlike all horoscopes.

The very next morning I received another affirmation that I had done the right thing in telling Elizabeth. My day's verse was Proverbs 3:5-6 "Trust in the Lord with all your heart and lean not on your own understanding; in all your ways acknowledge him, and he will make your paths straight."

This verse was the confirmation that God had used me as a tool in his cycle of help. This was undoubtedly a 'trust in God' moment - my understanding suggested I *not* tell her.

Then, by each party acknowledging him in the situation, the path to the result was clear and straight. Elizabeth told me she had tears in her eyes as she realised that this was a God thing, and it confirmed what she was thinking. Keith thanked me for helping and when I said it was a God thing, he agreed. He then gave God even more glory by sharing another story of how he had helped him.

There were four parties involved in this and *all* were blessed.

Let's take a look:.

Both mother and son:
- Became reunited with each other;
- Spent a lovely two days together;
- Were reminded of God's love for them;
- Saw God's love in action;
- Acknowledged and praised God for his handiwork.

Me:
- I had it confirmed that sharing the message was God's will, not mine, bringing me closer to him;
- Knowing that I was obedient and, got it right, I am more willing to act next time he asks;
- I receive a deeper clarity of his promptings each time

God:
- Received praise from all three of us mere mortals for his role in this;
- Saw a family reunited.

This is the Help-Save Cycle in process:

Need - a family separated, a mother worried about losing her son for good and a son missing having his mum in his life

Tool - he chose a person, me in this case, by making one sentence jump out in bold

Help - the help was communication, passing on a message that opened the restoration of a mother and son

Praise - three people praised God for his love and intervention (and potentially a lot more who have, and will hear the story)

Salvation - all three are at different stages of our love for God and have experienced very personal journeys in our relationship with Him, but this single event cements our salvation commitment.

In this case, God chose to share the outcome of his work with us, but we won't always see the results. Nor should we. That is as individual as the persons involved.

When you see an ambulance race past with lights and sirens flashing, you say a prayer for all involved, but you are not going to drive to the hospital and enquire of the outcome. Firstly, confidentiality restricts them from telling you. Secondly, it is none of your business. Likewise, the inner working of God on the heart of a person is none of your business.

It is always God's prerogative to decide whether to share information with us. If he decides to share, he has the right to decide what information he chooses to reveal to you. His decision is not based on anything more than our need to know for the purpose and outcome of that knowledge.

The patient in the ambulance is not going to draw closer to God by you knowing what physical injury they sustained. God determines our role and what he shares is totally up to him.

It may also be an unnecessary waste of your time to know. In business, details the manager of finance has will vary to the information the customer or salesclerk have. I stupidly quit a job once when I thought I was being shafted. I decided they were excluding me as part of their plan to sack me. But the truth is that I had no right, or reason, to know the information they were discussing.

Your job is to know God well enough to be able to hear his call and his instructions, not to play spy and try to work out all the details.

Key Points:
- Seeing the result is not the purpose of helping;
- Consider using a daily verse program;
- The Help-Save Cycle works;
- God determines our role and what we need to know;
- Your job is to know God well enough to hear his call and instructions.

Relationship and salvation: then and now

We don't usually set out to help another person purely so that they will go to heaven. Seriously, most people would label you a Bible-bashing preacher, or insane, if you told them that helping them move to a new house could get them to Heaven.

But it is okay to have the attitude of helping other people so that they will see the love of God and maybe begin to question their eternity and become saved.

But even that isn't the motivation I am talking about here. In fact, there are already books printed on witnessing and I am not addressing that either.

Keeping salvation as the eternal goal is about *you* obeying God and being used as *he* prompts you, asks you, demands of you, and expects of you. Whether it's your involvement in saving a life in a car accident, saving a new mother from her unforeseen tiredness, or giving money to a stranger, helping and salvation are not purely and obviously *spiritual*.

Please always keep in mind that God has a much bigger picture than what we could ever understand. He wants us in relationship with him while we are here on this earth and he wants us in heaven to spend eternity with him when that ends.

Throughout this book I hope you come to see how God uses our experiences to bless others and glorify him. For this purpose, he will allow us to go through certain trials. Would it surprise you to know that he would go to the point of killing us - for our own good, of course. God loves us so much that he would kill us to protect us! This concept seems foreign to the human mind, but you must understand that this is only a temporary body and that our spirits are *aliens* to this land, living in this world but being of God, longing for eternity in heaven with him.

"Because your heart was responsive and you humbled yourself before God when you heard what he spoke against this place and its people, and because you humbled yourself before me and tore your robes and wept in my presence, I have heard you, declares the Lord. Now I will gather you to your fathers, and you will be buried in peace. Your eyes will not see all the disaster I am going to bring on this place and on those who live here." (2 Chronicles 34:27-28)

There is a lot to be learned from the Garden of Eden and the eating of the forbidden fruit. We tend to forget that Adam was given an instruction and warned of the circumstances *before* Eve was created. Genesis 2:16-17 says, "And the Lord God commanded the man, "You are free to eat from any tree in the garden; but you must not eat from the tree of the knowledge of good and evil, for when you eat of it you will surely die."

In this case the result of the sin was known. God explicitly told Adam the rules and consequences of the actions that *he would* do. Sin entered the world as a result of this action.

I love the way God reacted to them in this story; the way he let them simmer. Let's read part of Genesis 3, verse 7: "Then the eyes of both of them were opened, and they realized they were naked; so they sewed fig leaves together and made coverings for themselves."

How long would that have taken? Several minutes at the absolute minimum! Even if they ripped off the nearest big leaves, *sewing* them together required stripping vine, cutting, stitching, then fitting the adornments to their bodies. Bear in mind, first they had to come up with the concept of clothing after this sudden revelation of shame. These two had never experienced the feeling of guilt, never considered or seen clothes and had no idea of sewing.

In verse 8: "Then the man and his wife heard the sound of the Lord God as he was walking in the garden in the cool of the day, and they hid from the Lord God among the trees of the garden."

Do you think God didn't know what happened? Of course, he knew. God lived with them and they talked every day. He is omnipresent. Yet here, when they commit their very first sin, he *slowly meanders* through the garden … in the cool of the day – late in the day.

Then in verse 9: "But the Lord God called to the man, "Where are you?"

God didn't need to ask them to tell him where they were. He wanted to give them the opportunity to respond. Parents, teachers and police use the same technique. Rather than telling the guilty what they have done, they ask for their version of events. The level of realisation, guilt and remorse are seen in the way a person responds. More than human authorities, God already knows the answers.

This was one experience that God wants us all to know about. But there will be times when you won't know the results.

We are told that some plant seeds, others water and other reap the harvest. Not everyone plays a role in the final step. We don't all see the competitors cross the finish line, but the supplier of shoes, the teachers and trainers, the spectators and so many others contribute to the outcome.

No, this is not another book about our responsibility to preach the gospel. It is another book about doing God's will. You can do God's will and let him do the preaching. Unlike you, he can get into their hearts, but you can cause them to open their hearts to hearing God, by *helping* him. That may be by baking a cake, driving a car, giving a smile, teaching someone to write a budget, praying with or for someone, or speaking to them about the gospel. Only God knows what each individual needs to have their heart opened for salvation.

A marriage is a union between two people who love each other. That love grows as they come to know each other. You want to be the one who knows your partner better than anyone else. And you trust in the fact that your partner knows you better than anyone.

In a marriage like this, you can speak for the other person. Decide for the other person. Act on behalf of the other person. I know very few couples that are this close all the time, but you definitely do not want anyone else in that position. Hence, wives often become jealous of the relationship between their husband and their work colleagues or their golf buddies.

But the relationship with God is one that we are not jealous about. We want everyone to enjoy that marriage, that union, that comfort of familiarity. The relationship we can have with God now is one that we want to share with others. So, in helping others, we want them to know that God had a part in it.

Though I too often fight it, I know that our relationship is much better when I get on my knees in humility and prayer. We get closer when I spend time talking with him. Reading the Bible and other literature also help me get to know God better. Then, and only then, am I able to know what he wants to do with me and through me.

Through constant discussion and commitment involving this unseen figure in my daily activities, I have a chance of living a life that is close to being the one that God created for me.

Now, let's look a little closer at a few verses from Psalm 119. "All your commands are trustworthy; help me, for men persecute me without cause … May your hand be ready to help me, for I have chosen your precepts … Let me live that I may praise you, and may your laws sustain me … Let my soul live, and it shall praise thee; and let thy judgements help me." (Psalm 119:86, 173, 175)

Like David, we are to make deliberate decisions and choose God's precepts. According to the Concise Oxford Dictionary, the word precept means: "Command; a rule of conduct; Moral instruction; A writ or warrant". Looking back at the original Greek word, the *Strong's Exhaustive Concordance* of the Bible tells us that the word 'pik-kood', means "appointed, ie a mandate from God, commandment, precept, statute."

David was asking for help from unwarranted persecution - something Jesus understands well. Therefore, God is going to be very understanding when his children call out with this prayer! Unfortunately, many people today are self-focused and see themselves as victims. This is not the kind of persecution David or Jesus endured.

God is talking about the persecution of his people, for his sake. To be persecuted for that you must be living in his word, and according to his commands and mandates - his precepts. David puts the two together: obey God's commands and God helps. The two cannot be separated. God is not out there to answer your every whim. He will not guarantee helping you if you are not living as he asked, no ... ordered, you to.

It is interesting how verse 175 has been watered down in the NIV translation. The NIV says "let *me* live and I *may* praise you." Whereas the KJV, the original English translation from the Greek and Hebrew Bibles, states "Let *my soul* live and it *shall* praise you." No if's, buts or maybes; it *shall*, it *will* praise you.

What will praise God? Maybe my big toes might dance in praise or maybe my arms might raise to you in praise. No! My *soul* – the part of me where the Holy Spirit lives. The part that guides my morals and convictions.

The part of me that will live eternally with God *will* praise him!

Key Points:
- Helping and salvation are not purely spiritual;
- God has a much bigger plan;
- God uses our experiences to bless man and glorify God;
- We want to share our God with others;
- Relationships improve by spending time together.

The goal - don't rush, wait on the Lord for direction

I hope you are starting to see that helping is not about witnessing. It is not about selfish gain. It is not about ... helping is about waiting on God's direction and, when he prompts you, to be obedient to do as he asks you to do.

On four occasions, I received letters calling me up for jury duty. This is something that excites me, but I still haven't served on a jury. Each time the case was cancelled, settled out of court or I just wasn't selected. But each time I was available. I had no idea who, or what, the cases were about. My only role was to attend where and when they told me to. The rest was totally out of my control. Obviously, if I was to be in that role of Juror, doing that job, my input would influence the outcome (more on that later) but, in the selection process, my only job was to be willing and able.

On each occasion, I needed to be prepared in case I was selected. To do this, I started by looking at my current lifestyle. My diary needed rescheduling and the household chores needed to be reorganised. I had to arrange for time off work, and select a book for the waiting room. There were things to do to facilitate my role. But my role, at that early stage was simply to hear the call and respond to it.

To hear a person call, we need to be listening. Phones on silent in another room tend to go unanswered. Likewise, to hear the call of God, we need to have a relationship with him so we are in a position to hear him talk. For me to hear the call to jury duty, I had to be in a position to hear. What good is the courthouse sending the letter to an address I have moved away from, or if I don't open my mail? The result of that is inconvenience, a waste of time and paper, an expectation gone unmet, and a fine to me. Not to mention, as I said earlier, I *want* to do jury duty, so I would also miss out on a blessing and all the joys, knowledge and growth from the experience.

Consider for a moment, Elizabeth's favourite Bible verse, Psalm 46:10: "Be still and know that I am God". It's one that is commonly quoted but broken down, it becomes even more powerful.

BE	make, allow, encourage yourself
STILL	quiet, at peace, calm, safe
AND	being still is nice, but not enough, 'and' implies there is more
KNOW	believe, trust, accept
THAT	used to indicate the aforementioned with the upcoming
I	God almighty, Father, Jesus, Spirit
AM	past, present, future, no maybes
GOD	maker of the universe, the one that loves you so much that he gave his son, so we can have relationship and eternity together.

Put together, he is calling us to stop, make him the focus, and then trust. This is not simple in the chaotic lifestyle we live, but it becomes easier with practice.

Until I started this study, I had no idea that there was a result to helping people. I thought it was a good thing to do and sometimes, if I verbally gave some glory to God, then someone may hear a bit about the gospel, and may put two and two together and realise that I was doing good because I love God. Hey, he's good, he can translate all that stuff in their heart, so they can work it out. I just need to be helpful. Right? As wrong as can possibly be!

There *is* a goal to helping. Do you think that God, who has laid out a plan for each of us, just wants us to be nice? Yes, that is a fruit of doing his will, but even the world wants niceness. The goal - the result - of helping God help others is that these others spend the rest of their life on earth knowing him, and doing his will. They then spend eternity in heaven praising him. That is the result – salvation for those who don't know him, a closer relationship with him for those who already do. So, as it is written in Proverbs 16:3 "Commit to the Lord whatever you do, and He will establish your plans."

How well we know a person initially is totally irrelevant, God knows them. So, irrespective of our relationship with other people, we can extend our compassionate duties to both family and strangers. That is our duty and responsibility, "So they can listen and learn to fear the Lord." (Deuteronomy 31:12)

Aren't we all strangers in this land? We live *in* this world, but our homes are heaven. We are not *of* this world; we are all aliens.

"For I was hungry and you gave me something to eat, I was thirsty and you gave me something to drink, I was a stranger and you invited me in, I needed clothes and you clothed me, I was sick and you looked after me, I was in prison and you came to visit me." (Matthew 25:35-36)

These are some of the most common types of help, all show practical and caring support. Notice how they were all delivered as needed, not before. The helper referred to here was not just doing it for the sake of doing it, nor for the accolades, and not because he thought it was a good thing to do. None of these things are considered big tasks, they should be commonplace. In fact, we are often taught to do good deeds and that is great. BUT…there is a responsibility to *do the good will of God, not the good ideas of humans.*

Helping others to help themselves is just as useful as giving them provisions, but do not rely on the messenger or your own instincts to know which way to best help which person. You have the responsibility to *wait on God and to obey his directions* when he tells you who to help, how and when. In the Deuteronomy verse above, we see the result is not to share the fruit amongst his people, the goal is so that the needy will *learn to fear the Lord.*

While you may be busy doing good, please apply the old saying, "Don't become so busy doing the work of the Lord that you neglect the Lord of the work."

Put Your Problems in God's Hands, by Helen Steiner Rice:
> *Although it sometimes seems to us our prayers have not been heard,*
> *God always knows our every need without a single word,*
> *And He will not forsake us even though the way is steep,*
> *For always He is near to us, a tender watch to keep…*
> *And in good time He'll answer us and in His love He'll send*
> *Greater things than we have asked and blessings without end…*
> *So though we do not understand why trouble comes to man,*
> *Can we not be contented just to know it is God's plan?*

Key Points:
- My job is to be available, to respond to his call;
- There is a purpose to helping other than the task at hand;
- There are things I can do to facilitate my role;
- Do the good will of God, not the good ideas of humans;
- God doesn't just want us to be nice.

Application for Chapter 2: The Purpose of Help

1. Give 2 reasons why God wants us to help one another?

   _____

   _____

2. Think of a time when you were motivated to help another person for selfish reasons. How would this event be different if God had asked you to do it?

   _____

   _____

3. Have you, or someone you know, had an experience when you have received help but didn't want people to know the details?

   _____

   _____

4. Think specifically about times you have helped another person. Briefly describe a time when you helped someone, and you saw the results. How did you feel? Who did you tell? What was your prayer?

   _____

   _____

   Now, Briefly describe a time when you helped someone,

and you didn't see the results. How did you feel? Who did you tell? What was your prayer?

_____

_____

Is there a difference?

_____

_____

5. Select one Bible reference mentioned in this chapter. Write it out on another piece of paper and put it on your fridge. Memorise it this week. What does this verse mean to you personally?

_____

_____

6. Has he given you any further insight into His plans for you? Write down an area that you have seen God at work in your life.

_____

_____

7. Spend some time talking to God about the things you have recorded in the questions above. Feel free to make any notes here that resulted from that prayer time.

_____

_____

SALVATION...

Chapter 3: God is the Example of Help

God helps us so we are able to help others. Paul expanded on this in 2 Corinthians 1:3-4. "Praise be to the God and Father of our Lord Jesus Christ, the father of compassion and the God of all comfort, who comforts us in all our troubles, so that we can comfort those in any trouble with the comfort we ourselves have received from God." In short, he comforts us, not just out of his love for us, but so we know how to comfort others.

God the Father is a helper

The Father helped us mere mortals by allowing his son to live on earth as a sacrifice so that we could come to know him personally and then spend eternity with him. Therefore, our eternity in heaven would not be possible without the love and help of God the Father. Agree? We simply could not get to heaven unless God devised the salvation plan and unless God allowed that to happen. We could not do it on our own. We *need* God's help.

It is good to also remember that he gave us a land that provides all we need - food, air and water to sustain us, and all the tools to survive and build a wonderful life here on earth. The earth that he made.

We are reminded in 2 Peter 1:3 that, "His divine power has given us everything we need for life and godliness through our knowledge of him who called us by his own glory and goodness."

Build a relationship with the Father

Now, just as earthly parents love to hear their children ask for help, the Father also loves to hear his children call to him for help. Sadly, too many people tend to call on God only when they are in trouble, using him as an emergency service contact, rather than someone they have a personal relationship with.

Remember, praying is for our benefit, not God's. He already knows exactly what is best for us, and what we will, and won't, ask for. He simply wants us to want him, need him, and thank him. Doesn't any parent?

As with any relationship, once we ask for help several times and realise that someone is willing to help us gladly and with no strings attached, our relationship with that person deepens. From this, the lines of communication become more frequently used, as we open up and learn to trust that person.

God is our refuge and strength

David, one of God's dear friends, reminds us that God is the one we run to when life gets tough. "God is our refuge and strength, an ever-present help in trouble." (Psalm 46:1). Note the phrase *ever-present help*.

God is not just there during our turmoil. He is not just a 'Santa Claus' waiting to deliver gifts when we ask. He is always there, always present, always next to us waiting for us to start up the conversation. Yes, he is our refuge, our hiding place, a safe place we can escape to.

He is also our strength; he gives us the peace, skills, whatever is needed to emotionally, spiritually, or physically get through whatever is placed before us. He is the ability that we don't have when confronted with trouble of any kind.

This might all seem so basic because you've heard it before, but please read on. I believe we often have to go back to the foundations before we can move forward.

If God wanted to remind us that he is always there to help us, why say he is an 'ever-present help'? Why not say he is a 'quick and resourceful' help? Speed is relative, sometimes the answers won't come as quickly as we would like and sometimes, they come in the most unexpected source.

Why use words such as 'refuge' and 'strength'? Because this is the type of *help* that he gives in times of trouble - refuge (safety) and strength (ability). God is, without a doubt, a refuge and strength.

He is the place we can run to when we need something. He is our hideout, a refuge where we can catch our breath again, a daddy whose arms we run to. What do you think of when you hear the word 'refuge'? I recall the women's refuge where women and their children can hide to catch their breath before moving into the next season of their life, a place where they are safe from the dangers of their husband or father. As men cannot get into a women's refuge, neither can our enemies penetrate God's protection.

I think of an island refuge in the middle of a road. After half of the journey - daunting, loud, dangerous and totally out of our control - we can rest and take a breath before the next part of the trip.

God is our refuge. We can hide in him, rest in him after a daunting period, gain our composure and strength for the next part of the journey. Then, he is the strength we gain. He is the ability, the breath, the strength we need to gather to get to, and through, the next phase of our life. Providing one or the other would be wonderful, but God doesn't do anything by halves. He gave us life and then he even gave us the Holy Spirit! He wants us to do more than live.

He is our strength, be it the emotional strength to carry on or the physical strength to persevere through the challenge. He is, and gives to us, every ounce of capability we need. He doesn't expect us to do this on our own. His goal is to help the people that he created, his children. He knows exactly what each child needs, how much, when and the best way to provide it. How can us mere humans possibly know all that? We can't.

Psalm 109:26 says it clearly, "Help me, O Lord my God; save me in accordance with your love." The KJV uses the word 'mercy' in place of 'love'. And what is the extent of God's love? He is unfailing in His love, eternal love, perfect love, ultimate love, practical love, disciplining love, never ending love, unbiased love, his endless mercy for us is … well … un-human.

To what extent then is God willing and able to help us? There is no end to the possibilities of what he can, and wants to, do for us.

Get to know God

Psalm 116:6 shows the interaction between the words 'help' and 'save'. The KJV says, "The Lord preserveth the simple: I was brought low, and He helped me." Whereas the NIV says, "The Lord protects the simplehearted; when I was in great need he saved me."

Did you notice the timing of God's addressing the need - when the author was "brought low" or "in great need". God allows us to go through times of need, bringing us to a low point in our lives (he would like us on our knees!) knowing what the result of that is - that we will call to him, and become closer to him.

That's not to say he can't or won't provide for us when our lives are going smoothly. But we notice more when things aren't going to plan. Even through the worst of times, God is calling out, and giving us opportunities, to get to know him better.

Psalm 54:4 says "Surely God is my help; the Lord is the one who sustains me." In this verse, David is being attacked by his enemies and he calls out for God to be his help. Verse 6 says, "I will sacrifice to you…praise your name." As helpers, we have the responsibility to offer sacrifices to him and to praise his name. What better sacrifice than you, your time, your mind, your heart, your kitchen…

Have you ever sent your sick child to school wondering whether they'll make it through the day - should you keep them home? Or have you ever kept them home only to have them fully recover by 9.30am? I got this wrong too many times. I would send one of them to school and get a phone call to come and collect them, but if I kept them home, they'd be fine by mid-morning. God doesn't have that problem. He *knows* what his children can and can't handle. He would never send them to school to have them come home sick (unless there was a separate lesson to be learned from the situation, we should never say *never* about God).

Parents who rush through the parental time may be fooled or guilted into certain decisions. Those who are able - and do - invest time with each child, learn to know them. They learn to read them, and know when things aren't as they seem. Quality time together pours resources into troubled times.

How well do you know your children? How well do they know you? Are they able to con a day out of school by pretending to be sick?

God the Father is never fooled. He knows every detail about every one of us, and he is in the ultimate and unique position to help everyone! He has access to every iota of information and resource available. We should never doubt his plans or ignore his instructions. We should trust it, and that trust comes through relationship with him.

I don't think the problem is accepting that God is a helper. I think the problem is trying to figure out what God wants us to do when he tells us he wants *us* to be helpers. I hope you are starting to discover how to *become the helper that God wants you to be.*

Key Points:
- Praying is for our benefit, to build our relationship with God. He already knows what we want and need;
- There is no limit to the love God wants to show us;
- God is our help;
- Get to know God so you can become the helper he wants you to be;
- Quality time together pours resources into troubled times.

God as Jesus is a helper

Jesus tells us in Luke 10:22 "All things have been committed to me by my Father. No one knows who the Son is except the Father, and no one knows who the Father is except the Son and those to whom the Son chooses to reveal him."

It was Jesus who suffered through those 33 years on earth and died the way he did. He suffered every temptation and pain so that he can honestly say "I understand" when we call to him for help. The result? Now Jesus intercedes for us, he represents us to God the Father. We no longer need a human priest - as in Old Testament times - with his limited understanding, knowledge of us and our experience, with no empathy and too much or too little sympathy. Jesus represents us honestly in his unique, ALL-knowing, ALL-loving way with no hidden agenda other than our best interests and our eternal salvation.

We read in 1 Peter 2:24, "He himself bore our sins in his body on the tree so that we might die to sins and live for righteousness; by his wounds you have been healed."

Psychologists and counsellors know that empathy helps more than sympathy. Having someone relate to what you're going through, rather than just pity you for going through it, is more personal, genuine and beneficial. Have you ever asked why you have been through so many horrible experiences in your life? Well, there's the "sin of the world" aspect, that is without doubt. I also believe that God allows (not causes, but allows) us to go through these things for a reason. That reason is simply, to bless man and to glorify God.

My kids probably got tired of hearing me say, "empathy over sympathy any day" - but they now use it, which means I said it enough. It brings a positive from a negative situation. It gives purpose to what you went through. It means God *chose you* to go through that exact situation because he could trust you to come out of it and would *bless man* (by having empathy and being willing to use it) and *glorify God* (by giving testimony of his greatness and being an example).

For those of you who are a bit unsure of the difference between empathy and sympathy, let me explain. Sympathy is feeling compassion or pity for the hardships of another, while empathy is putting yourself in the other person's shoes. Empathy is an emotional and knowledgeable understanding of the circumstances, where sympathy is looking from an outsider or distanced view, with little or no understanding of the situation. Remember, this is one of the reasons why Jesus lived on this earth as a man, to relate to what we go through.

His time, not our time

Jesus helped the hungry in their time of need by multiplying and providing the loaves and fishes. He did not waste his time serving food every day to every person. Instead, he saw their need and met their need when the time was right. **His time, not our time.**

This is one of the keys to being a helper - helping the people that God wants you to help, in the way that he wants you to help them, when he wants you to help them.

Most people eat every day. Just because it wasn't Jesus who fed them every day doesn't mean the people didn't eat every day. Helping doesn't mean doing all for all. It means being led by God to help those at the God-ordained time, place and way that will lead others to knowing God as their Saviour or, for believers, in a deeper way. What was the result of Jesus feeding the crowd? Thousands were spiritually saved, all were physically renourished, and mentally restored as well. This miracle wasn't just about food. Food was merely the tool he used to serve his purpose.

Can you imagine if Jesus decided that his job was to feed the multitudes? After all, that's a good thing to do, right? He would have invited guests to a fine dining experience, set up the tables of perfect food before greeting his guests and talking with them for hours. We would read a very altered history to the one we know. Probably one of humans being gluttonous and self-satisfying, then having a siesta during the sermon. I doubt much of the work that only Jesus could do, such as working miracles, would have been done.

Perfect timing

Time, as we know it, is irrelevant. Do you recall how long it took Jesus to get to Lazarus and to the dead girl? Jesus, as God, could have instantly moved himself to them (today's science fiction writers would probably use the term 'teleport'). He could have immediately healed them. So why do we read in John chapter 11 that he chose not to? Why would God ever delay in helping someone? Because he knew that there was more to be learned spiritually and eternally by delaying the task and allowing the people to go through the grieving and waiting.

Now, I'm not advocating procrastination here, but be sure that, in every situation, you wait upon the Lord for his instructions and, when you have them, act according to God's clock, not your own. The result, as with so many of his miracles, was that those who saw put their faith in Jesus, thus beginning their relationship with God and their confidence of eternity in heaven. Healing this human body is only a temporal winning. Bringing someone into relationship with God is an eternal win-win for all. Timing, however fast or slow it may appear to go, is perfected by God.

The terrorist attacks of 9/11 changed the world, but it has been reported that the number of employees delayed in getting to work that day was unusually high. I could never list all the miraculous interventions that saved lives that day, I can only mention a few. An unplanned office break, a broken shoelace, sleeping in, a late bus, a cancelled shift, holidays, wrong schedules, a changed route, a quick dash to the shops, a baby being born, and other family commitments.

While many of these survivors are still suffering the effects of that day, several have turned their life into a crusade to improve, repay, praise, and appreciate the life God has given them. Without wanting anyone to suffer, there are good things that come out of hard times.

In Hebrews 13:6 we are told "So we say with confidence, 'The Lord is my helper; I will not be afraid. What can man do to me?'"

Jesus, in praying for those who believe in him, said these words in John 17:26, "I have made you known to them, and will continue to make you known in order that the love you have for me may be in them and that I myself may be in them."

For a good understanding of what Jesus did for us, and our response to that, I urge you to listen to (or at least Google and read) the lyrics of the song, "We Are the Reason" by David Meece.

Key Points:
- Jesus has empathy, not just sympathy, for our circumstances;
- God chose you to suffer in this way for a purpose;
- Help who, how and when God wants you to;
- Helping doesn't mean doing all for all;
- There is more to learn by God's timing.

God the Holy Spirit is a helper

Throughout the Old Testament, the Holy Spirit was God's unseen anonymous helper on planet Earth. Zechariah 4:6 "'Not by might, nor by power, but by my Spirit', says the Lord Almighty." Then, in the New Testament, Jesus told his people that he was leaving the Holy Spirit for them, to operate through them to do God's will in this world. It wasn't long before his work became obvious.

God's gift to us

In John 14:15-17a Jesus says, "If you love me, you will obey what I command. And I will ask the Father, and He will give you another Counsellor to be with you forever - the Spirit of truth." Then in verse 26, "But the Counsellor, the Holy Spirit, whom the Father will send in my name, will teach you all things and will remind you of everything I have said to you." Interestingly, the noun used here has changed in the recent versions. The NIV says Counsellor, the New NIV says *Advocate* and the KJV says *Comforter*.

In the Old Testament, our guide for living generally came in the form of instructions, rules, or laws. It should come as no surprise then, that the word 'help' (and its associates such as helper, helped, helps) was used 178 times (NIV). In the New Testament however, it is only used 44 times (21 in the KJV).

Why the big difference? In the New Testament we have grace rather than laws, and we have been given the Holy Spirit rather than just priests. As a result, we have the fruit of the spirit, and spiritual gifts. So, the specific instructions to help are not required because helping is now a way of life; as a <u>fruit</u> and a <u>gift</u>.

Fruit: produce, the product or result of having the Holy Spirit living within and living the Christian life; being helpful;

Gift: personally selected, specifically targeted for a particular recipient; spiritual in nature; the helper or help provided.

Your talents, skills and gifts are God's gift to you. What you do with them is your gift to him.

Job 29:12 tells us that, "I rescued the poor who cried for help, and the fatherless who had none to assist him.". God has explained the importance of the fatherless, how he has put the responsibility on us to care for them because of the vast number of gaps left in their lives. In the famous Beatitudes (Matthew 5:3), Jesus told us "Blessed are the poor in spirit, for theirs is the kingdom of heaven." Then in 1 Timothy 5:5: "The widow who is really in need and left all alone puts her hope in God and continues night and day to pray and to ask God for help." The poor and the poor in spirit cry out to him.

Here, God puts the same emphasis on those who don't have someone to help them. Imagine, then, those people who are neglected because we neglect to obey God. God cares so much for each person, "that none shall perish", and "even the hairs of your head are known". How then, can he allow some to suffer without intervening and providing help? He doesn't. But, does the helper he chooses always obey? No. Therefore, instead of God's perfect will, we (the victims) are left with God's permissive will. His 'second best' if I may call it that.

In the Old Testament they didn't have the Holy Spirit. They came to God through the law, through works. Now, we don't have that human accountability, we have free will personified. Hence, today we see a lot more free sex, stealing, murder, unfaithfulness and so on. We may no longer be accountable to priests, but we are still accountable to God! To make a transformation in this world, just being good doesn't work. The power comes from the Holy Spirit to be ambassadors for God here on Earth.

The Silent Helper

Years ago, Jamie was on the verge of being in trouble as the clock raced and he couldn't find his school shoes. He was positive he had left them near the front door, but they weren't there. Or anywhere else he looked.

By being late, he missed the bus and his mother had to drive him the 20km into town. By being driven, Jamie wasn't on the bus that was involved in the accident that morning.

Now, we will never know what could have happened if he was on the bus that day, but I do know this: God loves us enough to protect us and he has a much bigger picture in mind then the location of a pair of school shoes.

When she returned home, his mother found the missing shoes - by the front door. Exactly where Jamie had declared he left them.

In between writing this section, I went to get changed for a birthday party. My 13-year-old daughter Kelly, wanted to pick my clothes, so she did that while I was in the bathroom applying the face paint.

"Mum," she called, "where are all your pants?"

I told her they were probably in the ironing pile or on the line. When I came out and put on the pants she had chosen, thinking they were a gift, I asked her where they came from.

"From your wardrobe," she replied.

"Yes, but where did they *come* from?" I know I forget things sometimes, but I have *never* seen these pants before!!!

I can tell you of many more miracles like this. Countless times, when I was a struggling single mum, I would be handed an envelope at the church door. These envelopes contained money that extremely generous members of my church family were giving to me. I have never once identified who gave the moneys, but I will never forget their gifts.

These givers, helpers, had no way of knowing what my financial circumstances were at the precise times of their giving. God did. Only God knew that there was an electricity bill due that week, or the car needed tyres for registration (and safety). God knew these things and chose tools, helpers, to solve my problems in my time of need. These gifts never arrived for me to go on a pleasure shopping spree, they were answers to problems.

I have no idea who give their money, or how many different people did. I have no idea whether God asked people that didn't obey, or what the relationships of the givers were with God. But I know that more than one person followed the promptings of God in helping me in my time of need. Now, to me, this money was a miracle. The timing and amount could have been no more obvious than if God himself had *magically* placed it in my hands. And, of course, he could do just that if he chose to. However, more blessings and praise are received by the Holy Spirit using people to bring about his plans.

Just because I know that there were people involved, doesn't mean God wasn't involved. It shouldn't take any of the glory away from him. Today, scientists can explain the Red Sea, but God was still the creator of that miracle. Even if you can 'justify' a miracle, don't lose sight of the fact that God orchestrated it, using his tools.

If those helpers are reading this, please know I am forever grateful that you chose to obey God's instructions. I pray that your blessings were as huge as mine. Thank you.

Jesus gave this command in Acts 1:4-5 "But wait for the gift my Father promised, which you have heard me speak about…you will be baptized with the Holy Spirit."

Baptised with - Jesus told us to be fully immersed with the Holy Spirit; to soak him in, to absorb the Holy Spirit into our life. This relationship is not the same as the one we have with the Father or with Jesus. This is not about *knowing* him, like we know Jesus. It is about *becoming one with him*, dying to self so that he lives through us. This is similar to the ideal marriage, where *your thoughts are my thoughts, your ways are my ways*. It is a lifetime commitment of living under the will and direction of another, rather than your own. Not as a slave, but in the peace of true love, as a child of God, in partnership with God the Holy Spirit.

By knowing him, we get to see that the Holy Spirit's passion is helping others. His *purpose* for being is to lead others to a closer relationship with God, the whole Trinity. We are his partner, his shell to work through. So, that means helping others becomes our passion as we get closer to him. You cannot know your friends' passions if you only talk to them once a year so don't think you'll know God's if you rarely speak to him!

Key Points:
- The Holy Spirit provides our spiritual fruit;
- The Holy Spirit is a gift - to us and for us;
- The Holy Spirit is our counsellor, advocate and comforter;
- The Holy Spirit empowers us to be ambassadors for God;
- The Holy Spirit operates his passion for helping through us as we work with him.

He made you like him

So, you've got the picture? God is a spirit, a loving heart wrapped in an outer case unlike the human body that we know. When he lived on earth as a man, Jesus experienced pain that very few of our bodies will know. But apart from those years, God's outer form is not like ours at all. Yet, God made man *in his image*. He made us to be a reflection of him, so others see him when they see us. That is not a physical resemblance as human families have.

That very same God is around, wanting to show his love to his people and the world. He can perform any miracle at any time, but he has chosen to use us to help in his work.

Take a moment to absorb that. God, the creator of the universe, is asking you to work with him on his plan for humanity.

Right from the very beginning, God was revealing his character and his longing to help his people and his other creations. To this end, and because we are made *in his image*, he wants us to help also. We are a part of God's creation and this is his desire, so he has led the way by setting the example for us to follow.

I accept God as being the Holy Trinity, as one in three divine beings. I don't think it a coincidence, in fact it is commonly accepted, that people are threefold, with body, mind and spirit. The number three is considered a symbol of perfection. It is used in many aspects. The Chinese identify there are 3 stages of life - birth, marriage, death. Writers believe in the rule of three as a principle for readers to remember information. Actors and artists divide their work areas in three sections.

God, as always, is all things to all people. And all things to all aspects and experiences of all people. It is up to us to have a relationship with him whereby we are capable of hearing and being aware of his workings.

Why? Why doesn't God just zap His miracles? He can. I've seen it with the school shoes, pants and keyring. But if he chose that method of getting things done, we'd become even more complacent, selfish and distant from him and humans wouldn't recognise their need for him. Then, others wouldn't recognise him when they look at us. Besides that, the blessing we receive when we are part of giving to someone else cannot be beaten. God always knows the bigger picture, things we will never know.

When her grandmother moved into a nursing home, Cherie felt she was unable to help. What she did do was take on a responsibility that no one else had even thought about - managing the financial concerns of this elderly lady.

Cherie paid the bills, cancelled unused subscriptions, and balanced her bank accounts. She followed up on the incorrect transactions of overcharged medications and room fees. She ensured that her grandmother was in the position to receive the best care possible.

To Cherie, this seemed only a simple act. Because this is what she does for work, it took less time and effort than it would if anyone else had done it.

God used a combination of the skills Cherie had learned, with the heart he had given her, and produced a result that no other member of the family could have. With her willingness to be available, God was able to work through her to act as he would in this situation. He made her like him.

Share your road map

Do you know that the journey you have travelled is even more important than the location you arrive at? The Israelites wandered through the wilderness for 40 years. On many occasions, I compare myself to these self-centred, rebellious, short-sighted Israelites who kept going from blessings to sins regularly. They seemed to forget the miracles so quickly - as I have so often. Moses reminded them in Deuteronomy 28:45-47 "All these curses will come upon you.....as a sign and a wonder to you and your descendants forever. Because you did not serve the Lord your God joyfully and gladly in the time of prosperity."

Yet, reassurance comes in 2 Peter 3:9, "The Lord is not slow in keeping his promise, as some understand slowness. He is patient with you, not wanting anyone to perish, but everyone to come to repentance."

They wasted 40 years and yet we know their story, their experiences. Why? Because God teaches us things even in our mistakes and failures. We need to be willing to learn these lessons and share them with others.

What is the eternal good here?

First, I have another illustration of the Holy Spirit intervening in our lives.

I had become a frequent commuter for a few months and experienced the tide of full and empty train carriages. One day, as I boarded the almost full train, a woman moved across her seat from aisle to window position, giving me the only available seat in the carriage.

I thanked her then commented on the book she was reading. It was a Christian book, so I assumed she was a Christian. She pulled another one out of her bag and told me to keep it. This book was called *Loved Back to Life* by Sheila Walsh.

Apart from the book, the miracle was in the way we met. Just as I entered the carriage, God told her to move over. She heard the inaudible but clear voice telling her when to pick up her bag from the seat and slide across. *Just* in time for me to sit down.

We struggled to talk in the Quiet Carriage but knew we had a connection, and so we exchanged contact details.

As the days went on, I sent her an email thanking her again for the book, now finished. The content of this book was exactly what I needed and the timing was perfect. Only God knew my story and how the *black dog* was biting at that time. This book still has more post-it notes than any other book in my library.

When I heard nothing from her, I named my friend my 'Train Angel', convinced that I was the only one who saw her that day.

Proverbs 16:9 tells us that "In his heart a man plans his course, but the Lord determines his steps." I planned to get on that train, but God filled in the details with a seat, a new book and a special friend.

Do you ever pray for a car park and get one? I have, countless times. If you're one of these God-dependant drivers, have you ever stopped to consider the intervention required to get you that car park? have you thought about how many steps God must determine before we even know we want that carpark. And, if you are like me, your request usually gives him no more than a minute's notice.

Think about it: you had to leave your last location (work or home) at a certain time to arrive here right now. Depending on where you are travelling, the traffic plays a huge part in determining the precise second you arrive – the timing of the lights changing and the length of the queues. Every person in that queue had to leave their last location at a precise time. I know I couldn't coordinate that, only God could.

Then, the person departing the car park you are about to enter had to get up, leave, go through their day in the perfect time, just to leave this location right now when you need their carpark. What if their child was slow (or fast) or they received a phone call? Does this make you think that even those minor inconveniences are a part of God's overall plan? And I've only mentioned what's happening outside the store. The person leaving your car park had interactions of differing time lengths. Their getting back to their car depended on the speed of the shopkeepers and customers, the length of the line-ups, the time spent browsing inside each store that person entered.

Now, how important is it that you get *that* carpark *now*? Not very. But that's how much God loves you and that's how helpful the Holy Spirit is!

Key Points:
- Being in God's image does not refer to physical attributes;
- God wants to work through us to act as he would in any situation;
- God's timing is perfect;
- Like the trinity, we are three-fold: body, mind and spirit;
- God made you to help others.

Application for Chapter 3:
God is the example of Help

1. What are some key differences between the help of God:

   The Father _____

   Jesus _____

   Holy Spirit _____

2. In what ways are you like God:

   The Father _____

   Jesus _____

   Holy Spirit _____

3. Write down 3 miracles that God could instantly perform. Next to each, write a blessing or lesson that would be missed if he did that.

   _____

   _____

   _____

4. Recall a time when you went through a rough time and wanted a 'quick fix' solution. In hindsight, what did you learn / what strength did you gain from that experience?

   _____

5. Select one Bible reference mentioned in this chapter. Write it out on another piece of paper and put it on your fridge. Memorise it this week. How can this verse change your way of seeing your relationship with God?

_____
_____
_____

6. Write 3 areas of your life where you would like to be more like God.

_____
_____
_____

7. Pray about what you have read, written and thought about today. Feel free to make any notes here that resulted from that prayer time.

_____
_____
_____

Part 2: Salvation THROUGH…

In the Belief-Expectation Cycle we were told, "Changing your expectation changes your attitude". Your expectation of God's purpose for you may be this - attend church, read the Bible, pray regularly and be good. What about his work here on earth, what's your role in that? Do you take God along with you, or do you just call on him when you are stuck or in trouble? I challenge you to consider allowing God to work through you. To be available and expect him to have his way, doing his work, through you.

God chose to use people as one of his methods of helping other people through their time of need. God chose to help others through you. He could bypass you to work miracles, but that would leave you out of the miracles, the blessings, the growth, the training, the …

God needed someone who would not take the pity road or expect the glory, but would use their experiences to help others (bless man) and do it humbly (glorify God). Someone who would take their experiences, skills, knowledge and love for him and allow him to use these for a specific purpose. And for that exact purpose, God chose *you*. He chose to work *through* you.

Have you ever looked back and wondered why you were the one to go through that experience? Well, consider yourself privileged that you did. Yes, privileged. Please don't consider me thoughtless here, quite the opposite. I am thinking of all the other people that are, and will, go through the exact situation that you say you wouldn't wish upon your enemies. At some point, they will have you to help them through it. And I hope that you have, or had, someone when you experience your rough times. Empathy beats sympathy every time, remember.

If we step back and try to consider the world as God does, we acknowledge that there is always a bigger picture. And while absolutely every person matters, we know that there will always be an incomprehensible number of people who suffer through an event that the victim thinks they are alone in. And who best to help console, support and help the sufferer than one who genuinely understands the process and symptoms, because they have lived through it. That's why I say it is a privilege to suffer, because your suffering can bring help to others in their time of suffering, making your experience, dare I say it - worth it. God wants people in his toolkit. We will look at preparing yourself to be his tool so he can work through you.

Salvation THROUGH...

Chapter 4: In God's Hands

You probably know the chorus to the children's song, "He's got the whole world in his hands..." What do you do with things you hold in your hands? Do you hold a baby and a can of paint the same way? I hope not. God wants us to delicately and personally look at your position in his hands as we learn to replicate that responsibility.

Heading for heaven

We know God wants to help his people through the hard times. He never intended to leave us alone on this earth; that's why he gave us the Holy Spirit. Unfortunately, there are still a lot of people who have not made a decision for Christ and it is our responsibility, as Christians, to reach them.

Do you find yourself longing for the day when we are living in heaven with the Lord? I'm sure he is longing for that same day. However, he waits with frustration because he knows that we have the ability to cause that day to come sooner.

He told us in Matthew 24:14, "And this gospel of the kingdom will be preached in the whole world as a testimony to all nations, and *then* the end will come." He cannot come until every man, woman and child has had the opportunity to make a decision for him.

He also told us that we have a responsibility to preach the gospel so that others can have that opportunity. Romans 10:14 says, "How, then, can they call on the one they have not believed in? And how can they believe in the one of whom they have not heard? And how can they hear without someone preaching to them?" So, if we don't preach, others cannot have the opportunity to be saved and, until everyone is given that opportunity, God will not come back for us.

Turn that around and we see that as soon as *we* have given everyone in our path the opportunity to accept Christ as their Saviour, then Christ can return, and we get to start living eternity in heaven with God. What are we waiting for?

God doesn't expect everyone to accept Christ but, because of his love, he insists that everyone has the choice. So, don't be discouraged if you don't convert everyone to following Jesus, that transition is between them and God. You need to simply *do your job*.

Your job starts at the temple. "Then Zerubbabel son of Shealtiel and Jeshua son of Jozadak set to work to rebuild the house of God in Jerusalem. And the prophets of God were with them, helping them." (Ezra 5:2). As they should have been! It wouldn't be right if people tried to build God's temple and God's chosen people were not there to help. Unfortunately, that often happens.

We have been told that our bodies are the temple of the Holy Spirit and we have been entrusted with them. Once we accept that, we should try to build our bodies, his home, to be the strongest and most suitable house in the best way - spiritually, physically, emotionally and mentally.

Now, if *my* body is the temple of the Holy Spirit, it means that the bodies of *other* Christians are the temple of the Holy Spirit. Therefore, we have responsibility for how we treat other people, God's temple, the church – which is the body of Christ.

In this passage, the house of God was being *rebuilt*. God doesn't give up on us if we get it wrong the first time, he graciously gives us a chance to rebuild. In fact, there are so many more opportunities to get it right the second-time round. Making mistakes has certain advantages – not that I recommend that as the benchmark.

Like building a church, salvation doesn't just happen. God uses vessels, tools, words, deeds … Jesus used parables, miracles, teaching … We are merely one of his methods. What's more, we are not in control, God is. This is the life *he* gave me, and he has it all under control. Jesus made sure of that, "Just as the Son of Man did not come to be served, but to serve, and to give his life as a ransom for many." (Matthew 20:28). Jesus set the ultimate example of how we should love and help the people that he puts in our lives.

Not I, you say. *Who am I to think that I could possibly work for the Great God Almighty?* We all have moments of doubt regularly. I tell myself, I*'m not a missionary;* or *I couldn't possibly be worthy;* or *How can I be of any use, I've wrecked my life; Look at the mistakes I've made.*

Fact: It's not about me, it is *God's will* that we become helpers for *his work* to be done.

Fact: He will provide the tools, the desire and the directions.

Fact: God is so gracious that he allows us to use the mistakes we make as teaching tools – they offer experience, understanding and empathy.

You MUST have relation with God while doing his work.

"Remain in me, and I will remain in you. No branch can bear fruit by itself; it must remain in the vine. Neither can you bear fruit unless you remain in me. I am the vine; you are the branches. If a man remains in me and I in him, he will bear much fruit; apart from me you can do nothing." (John 15:4-5). There is so much in these two verses.

'Remain in me'. This is a call to constant relation. If you plant something and neglect it, you will get little fruit, no fruit, or fruit that is sick and diseased and flavourless. If you remain in the vineyard (or garden), watching and caring for your plants, you will produce abundant healthy tasty fruit.

When I reignited my interest in having a vegetable garden, I went straight out and bought a replacement copy of the *Yates Garden Guide*. I had one of these books 30 years ago and knew that its content gave me all the instructions and motivation I needed to grow healthy vegetables, flowers, trees and shrubs. It is my go-to for anything related to the garden.

I sat for hours with this book, pen, paper and a coffee. I sketched, planned and wrote list after list. This book fine-tuned my skills and increased my motivation to create the garden we would be happy with. It also prepared me to know what resources I needed to obtain from other experts.

All of this planning was only relevant to the garden I have now. My garden is different to any other garden. Every garden is unique. Every garden has a different purpose, time frame, history, climate and each will weather the weather differently. But the true gardener will know his garden completely. Not just the textbook facts, but his individual plants. He knows how the shade appears at particular times of the year, where the weeds grow and when. He knows when it needs more mulch, more water or fertiliser than the recommended dose.

This is the difference between knowing about and knowing, or between surviving and living. God is the greatest gardener and he knows each of us 'plants' intimately. After all, he made the Garden of Eden before he made us.

The key is having a relationship with your subject - whether that is a plant, a garden, your child, your partner, your boss or God. You *must* have relation with God while doing his work. When doing the work of the Lord, don't forget the Lord of the work. When helping the people of your Lord, don't forget the Lord of the people.

The word 'fruit' does not refer only to those healthy foods that grow in gardens or vineyards. Biblically, fruit is anything that is a product of effective prayer in Jesus' name. We derive life from Jesus, and He produces fruit through us.

We can do nothing without the help of God. He provides every means to do every task. He can give, or take, our very breathe away (physically and metaphorically). We deserve no credit at all. We are here because of him, and for him.

Jesus tells us that the Father trims clean every branch that bears fruit, so it will produce even more fruit. Pruning is good for plants. Pruning is good for us. When God prunes us, he makes us kind, patient and ready. It may hurt, and we may look funny for a while, but the benefits far outweigh the temporary discomfort and embarrassment.

Being prepared (willing) to do what he asks is not the same as being prepared (able) to do what he asks. I need to know what he wants and be willing to do his plans instead of mine.

On multiple occasions in the Bible, God chose to use those people - tools - who were less than capable in the eyes of man, like David or Mary. He reduced armies so they would appear incapable of winning, so he would get the glory. So, by inference, we who are the weakest are perhaps the most usable.

We are the human, fallible, off-track version of the interpretation God made of himself, with nearly 7,000 years of unskilled variations. God does not expect us to be perfect, he simply calls us to be available.

Key Points:
- When helping the people of the Lord, don't forget the Lord of the people;
- You can speed up God's return by helping with his work;
- Being prepared (willing) is different to being prepared (able);
- Being pruned is good for us;
- We, the weakest, are perhaps the most usable.

Trust and be Thankful

Take a moment to think about what God has provided for you already. In 1 Chronicles 22:17-18 "David also commanded all the princes of Israel to help Solomon his son, saying, is not the Lord your God with you? And hath He not given you rest on every side? For He has given the inhabitants of the land into mine hand; and the land is subdued before the Lord, and before His people."

God has this whole thing in his hand. We may not see the results immediately, but we can certainly depend on him to provide. He wants us to help others as he has helped us. No matter what you are facing, believe that the Lord is with you, directing you, has your best interests at heart and has gone before you to prepare your victory.

When my husband made the decision to leave me, I struggled with the fact that he had decided to leave but took his time in doing so. Then, one day the Lord pointed out to me that my husband had, "claimed his freedom but not yet moved into it." That's what we all have to do: acknowledge that God has prepared our freedom for us, and then move into it. Take the next step to claim that victory.

Faith is trusting that God will bring the results, and because of this, we can *thank him in advance.* However, trusting in God is *not an excuse to do nothing.* We can't just sit back and expect him to do it all for us. This is not because he is a demanding parent, but because he is a loving one. Think of the skills and experiences your life would lack if you hadn't lived through each day of your life.

I am saddened by the amount of time that a lot of our technology-age kids spend on their gaming consoles and computer gadgets. Worse still is the lie that this is exercise. Some naïve parents even say, "at least they are playing some sport, and it's good for their hand-eye coordination." I strongly disagree.

Holding a computerised controller to hit a tennis ball does not compare to having the wind blow in your face, the heat beaming on the back of your neck, the weight of the racquet, the power behind the ball when it flies towards you, the twang of the strings as the two connect, or the exhilaration of personal pride as you land that tennis ball in the court beyond the net. Not to mention the sportsmanship skills that come from waiting for a court, saving for your own racket, winning and losing against friends and foe.

There is so much more to be gained from going through an experience. This is one of many reasons why God chooses *not* to automatically, magically, instantly answer our prayers in the most obvious human-like method. Trusting God is what we do when we have done everything else that he wants us to do.

Here is a story that shows that God doesn't want us to idly depend on him. Commonly referred to as, "The Drowning Man", it has been recreated in various forms and levels of severity, but this version was found in Truthbook.

A fellow was stuck on his rooftop in a flood. He was praying to God for help. Soon a man in a rowboat came by and the fellow shouted to the man on the roof, "Jump in, I can save you."

The stranded fellow shouted back, "No, it's OK, I'm praying to God and he is going to save me." So the rowboat went on.

Then a motorboat came by. "The fellow in the motorboat shouted, "Jump in, I can save you."

To this the stranded man said, "No thanks, I'm praying to God and he is going to save me. I have faith." So the motorboat went on.

Then a helicopter came by and the pilot shouted down, "Grab this rope and I will lift you to safety."

To this the stranded man again replied, "No thanks, I'm praying to God and he is going to save me. I have faith." So the helicopter reluctantly flew away.

Soon the water rose above the rooftop and the man drowned. He went to Heaven. He finally got his chance to discuss this whole situation with God, at which point he exclaimed, "I had faith in you but you didn't save me, you let me drown. I don't understand why!"

To this God replied, "I sent you a rowboat and a motorboat and a helicopter, what more did you expect?"

Trusting God and leaving it all to him is like knowing the plants are dry and, instead of watering them, you watch from the window while praying for rain. We need to do our bit, play our part, live up to our responsibilities. Then God can, and will, do the rest. What glory does God get, and what message does it send to others, if we are lazy. We don't want people searching for God, or new Christians following our idleness and expecting he will fix everything. He can, but we want them to understand that he loves them, and that their life has a purpose.

So, whether the plants are dry, or the house is flooding, the first question should be, God what do you want *me* to do?

God's resourcefulness means he can use the same action for a multitude of purposes. We are told in Job 37:13 that, "He brings the clouds to punish men, or to water his earth and show his love." Likewise, he can use the same situation to help those in it, but in very different ways.

I am sure you have been on both sides of helping and both sides of gratitude, or lack thereof. You've helped someone and been thanked. You've helped someone and not been thanked. You've thanked someone for helping you. You've not thanked someone for helping you (maybe you didn't have the opportunity or, were simply distracted. We're all human). While the "thank you" is never the motive to help another person, it is nice to hear it. In most people, it puts a smile on our face and creates a little joyous butterfly in our stomach.

The word 'appreciate' has different meanings: you can appreciate what someone else has done, or you can appreciate the situation someone else is in. Showing appreciation can take many forms:
- Simply say, "Thank you for your help, it really meant a lot".
- Send a thank you card and / or gift. Don't make it elaborate so the attention is back on you. Make it personal so the focus is them.
- Saying a heartfelt verbal, "Oh thank you God for keeping the rain away until we finished." This is not Bible-bashing, just say it honestly as you would say it silently, but say it out loud.

By being an appreciative person, you are:
- Appreciating and acknowledging God's role in this situation;

- Humbling yourself away from being the centre of attention;
- Leading by example and helping others to appreciate others;
- Showing that helping is not something that should be taken for granted.

Please be mindful though, that some people cannot handle the attention and do not know how to respond. They may choose deliberately not to be available for the acknowledgment, to avoid the presentation, or to remain anonymous. Some even react with apparent anger at the situation or involvement of another. That is their choice. Don't try to change them, just concentrate on changing you!

I was walking into a supermarket one day when I couldn't help but hear a lady crying on the phone. She was telling the listener about her misfortune with money. Sorry, I cannot recall all the details, but it got my attention and pulled at my heart. This woman desperately wanted a haircut (possibly before a wedding or something big event) but through circumstances beyond her control, she was left desolate. Her call ended just as we arrived at the doors and that was my confirmation to act. I opened my wallet and handed her a $50 note. I could argue that I couldn't afford it but, at that time, she was much needier than I was. Needy financially. Needy emotionally. Needy spiritually. She needed comfort. She needed reassurance that her life wasn't worthless. She needed love. She needed God.

Receiving is not easy, it's embarrassing and can be humiliating, but I knew God was prompting me to do this and he doesn't embarrass people. As I put it in her hand, her look was pure gratitude. What do you say when someone gives you those astounded eyes? Simply, "Thank God".

I didn't hang around. She was obviously overwhelmed, and I didn't want to embarrass her. At other times, I have noticed someone in distress and their need is a closed office door and a shoulder to cry on. Colossians 3:17 tells us "And whatever you do, whether in word or deed, do it all in the name of the Lord Jesus, giving thanks to God the Father through him."

Key Points:
- Faith is thanking God in advance for what we cannot yet see or understand;
- Everyone in every situation is different;
- Trusting in God is not an excuse to do nothing;
- There is much to be gained from going through a bad experience;
- Be appreciative and lead by example.

He wants humans, not robots

God's goal is for us to get closer to him, even if that's not always our goal! Earlier, I noted that God can leave us out of his work, but that we benefit so much by being involved in it. Can you say that about your day job? Do you benefit by being there and doing your work? Or are the owner and the customers the only ones that seem to get anything out of it?

Rest assured that God understands the process of work. He instilled it in Adam and Eve, gave people skills and talents, as well as instructions to build.

While there is an end goal to manufacturing clothes or doing someone's tax, the end product is not the only factor. The employee learns new skills to do their job, they fine tune those skills by putting them into practice, becoming an experienced, valuable asset in that field. That person can apply those skills in different projects and workplaces. God too can use that person in future similar situations. And don't underestimate the feel-good factor of accomplishing a task, of seeing a result, of helping someone out of a problem.

Years ago, I was an Employment Consultant in the very cold town of Armidale, and I helped a lot of people find jobs. One male had been in his new job for just over a week, all paperwork completed, and I did not expect to see him again. But I will never forget the day he came in and asked to see me. Talking about his new job, he finished with these words, "Thank you Sandi, I can now buy firewood to warm my family."

What I had done was nothing special. In fact, I was paid to do it. It was my job. But here was a man who understood and appreciated the role I played in his life changing. *If God's only purpose for a task was the result, then he would have made robots rather than humans.*

Consider the benefits from even those tasks that seem menial, such as helping a child with their homework. Not only do you get the feel-good factor of seeing your child advance, but you get the pride of knowing you recalled something you learned many years ago. You also get to spend quality time with your child, you see the stress go from them, and experience their appreciation of your time.

It was made clear in 1 John 4:11, "Dear friends, since God so loved us, we also ought to love one another." Verse 16 goes on to say, "And so we know and rely on the love God has for us. God is love." Then verse 17 summarises it, "because in this world we are like him."

As humans, we try to use logic when talking to God, but do yourself a favour, know that he is much more powerful than the words our logic could ever conceive! When I was 18, he gave me the prophecy that I would have the gift of help. A year later, my mother went on a holiday to Hawaii and brought me back a gift, a keyring - and not just any keyring. Firstly, I hadn't even realised at that stage that I collected these things. Secondly, it was the words on it that were so important. Thirdly, I was in for a lesson.

The front of the keyring read: **Sandra ~ Kani ~ Helper**

In the language of Hawaii, the word 'Sandra' is translated as 'Kani' which means 'helper'. I was majorly impressed, but God already knew this. In fact, he worked that out *long* before there ever was a Hawaii or a Sandra!

As a side note, I later went on to name my first business Kani Consultants, the name has been used for many codes and our first daughter was very nearly named Kani. The name just entered my heart.

On the back of the keyring was an acronym for the word Sandra, all with words relating to being a helper, though I have no idea what they were. You have no idea how much I would love to be able to include the words here. There was my very first lesson in obeying the voice of God. The lesson went like this:

My mother gave me the keyring, I had a couple of days to read it, memorise it and grasp the concept of God's miracles and how he co-ordinates the whole world together for us little beings. After a couple of days, I was sleeping soundly one night when I suddenly woke with God saying to me, "Sandra, write down the words that are on the keyring."

How did I respond? Well, how did Jonah or David respond, yep I'm stupid too! "Okay God, I'll do that. I'll do it first thing tomorrow, good night."

"Sandra, write down the words that are on the keyring." It always amazes me how God's voice can be stern while still so loving, but again I put my own selfish human thoughts first. "Lord I am so tired now, I know exactly where it is, it can't get lost. It's attached to my keys, in my handbag, on my dresser. I promise I will do it tomorrow."

Don't you just love (ha ha) the way we use the word 'Lord' when we are saying 'No' to God. I mean, that has got to be one of the biggest contradictions of all time! Anyway, you've got the idea, three times he tried to get me simply to get up, get the keyring and write down the words of the acronym on the back of it. Easy, right? Except that I chose to be disobedient.

The next morning, not feeling at all refreshed, I went to do what God had told me to do during the night. I went to my dresser, opened my handbag and pulled out my cluster of keys. Can you imagine how I felt when the keyring wasn't there? The keys were, just not the keyring.

I went through all the logical thoughts - when did I last see it, where could it have fallen off, what happened to it, and came to only one conclusion: God removed it after my act of disobedience.

After my feeble attempt at repentance, I tried to recollect the poem, the acronym, the words that typified what God had told me he'd make me. To this day, I still cannot recall them. It's like he has deliberately put a block on that part of my memory. And yet, I thank him. The keyring I cannot take to heaven. The words on it made me a little closer to Him, but the lesson made me a *lot* closer to him. Now, I am *not* in any way advocating disobedience. The hurt it causes is very unpleasant. And sometimes, we are still too thick to learn the lesson and must go through it multiple times. Just realise that he is in everything - and don't think logic will win.

For the record, I went on to collect nearly 200 keyrings, but I still yearn for that one. I am more than grateful to have learnt that valuable lesson and, if I still had that one today, I wouldn't have had *that* opportunity to learn about obedience. There would have, and have been, plenty of other opportunities, but in true

God-like form, that one was perfect and very meaningful - and it brought me closer to Him, which is the goal with all that he does.

Subconsciously, this event stayed with me, and I started to accumulate many more of this little plastic and metal toys from holidays, and I even received them as gifts. I would put them on my keys and, as they got too heavy, I would remove them and stash them in a drawer somewhere, before buying more. Several years later, during a move, I started to gather all the bundles into one and realised that I had over 60 keyrings! At that point, I realised that I was a collector and went on to collect over 200 before giving them to my son. Two of his children now collect them - Melissa because they are pretty and Archer because he's like his nanna and dad.

God could have used any tool to implement this message for me. He chose a square piece of plastic to teach me to listen to him and be willing to act on his promptings.

Remember that God encourages us into action, he doesn't force us. Robots, however, are not malleable. They act the same, hear the same and react the same. Every time. It has been said that a multitude of people can be in the same room at the same time and hear the same words, yet each of them will take home a different account of the event. This is because we are all a product of our past and present experiences, combined with our knowledge and associations, plus our beliefs and ... you get the picture. We are unique.

So, for God to be able to work through us, he needs access to our individuality that separates us from the pack. That is the Spirit inside of us. It is his Spirit that he wakens and spurs into action when he wants to talk to us. So, when you hear the same as everyone else hears but something jumps out at you and you know that part of the message is for you, act on it - because it is very possibly the Lord God trying to tell you something.

Can you recall the story of the mother and son, Elizabeth & Keith? God chose to use my mouth as the tool to funnel that message from son to mother for him to then do the repairs. A robot would have simply heard all the words the same, but the spirit in me was able to pick up on the message and task at hand. The result of this was the salvation of a mother and son's relationship and God getting the glory.

Key Points:
- Our skills become assets usable in multiple situations;
- The words 'Lord' and 'no' cannot go together;
- God's lessons draw us closer to him;
- Value the lessons we learn when we make mistakes;
- Listen out for the differences that robots cannot hear.

Imagine having the power of the Holy Spirit in you!

Take heed of the words in 1 Peter 4:11b, "If anyone serves, he should do it with the strength God provides, so that in all things God may be praised through Jesus Christ. To him be the glory and the power for ever and ever. Amen." Again, *bless man* - by serving and doing good things - and *glorify God* - by giving him the praise in the situation.

God has already told us not to use our power. He does not expect, or want, us to use our own limited abilities, tools, strength or insight. Why would we, when we have access to the one with the omnipotent power? God merely wants us to be the vessels through which he does his work. Why? Because he alone can do the job properly and, *"So that in all things God may be praised through Jesus Christ"*.

Not only does he do the job better than us, God doesn't leave us alone to do his work. For him to work *through* you, there must be a channel of sorts.

We sing songs about being in his hands, and that is a beautiful image. But I believe that, when it comes to us being his helper, the system is more like the garden hose. He wants to water his garden and we are the hose that he holds to enable his power to flow through to reach the living object in need of help. God is the gardener, the people are the plants, we are the hoses, and the Holy Spirit is the water .

As much as we often like to think we know all about all, news flash - we don't. Only he knows all the details of every situation, and only his love and motives are 100% pure. We can easily be tricked into thinking that not doing certain things makes us good and holy, but it's actually the opposite! It's doing *something* that makes us faithful followers of Jesus!

The danger for most of us is not that we'll become bad people who don't care about things that matter. No, the danger is that we'll become good people who don't do anything that matters!

Within you lies a person who desires to love. God's spirit is pulling you and inviting you to become more of that person. The spirit never guilts you, shames you, or bullies you to become more loving. He compels you! I can muck up God's plan by mismanaging this toolbox, but as I grow and know God better, I put my tools in his capable hands.

Can you imagine truly claiming the words of Acts 1:8 where we are told, "You will receive power when the Holy Spirit comes on you..." Power to do what God called us to do. Not physical strength. Not magical powers. Not strong minds. But the ability to do God's will, to carry out his plans, to be the shell that the Holy Spirit can live through to do his work on earth in this age of grace.

Take a moment and think about the Holy Spirit.
- He is God
- He works miracles
- He was given to us by Jesus
- He is all-knowing
- He is all-present
- He is an intercessor for us to God the Father
- He dwells in believers
- He works in us to do God's will
- He is a teacher
- He is our guide
- He gives abundant life
- He is the comforter
- He brings Christ's words to remembrance
- He convicts the world of sin

Feel free to write down anything I have missed:
_____
_____

And. He. Wants. To. Operate. Through. YOU!

Imagine for a moment that you are an Amway Representative. How would you react if and the world's number one sales representative decided he wanted to be in your team? Would you say no? Would you honestly tell him to go and join another team? Would you tell him that you didn't want his masterful expertise and experience on your side, that you didn't want to reap the benefits of his sales abilities? I don't think so. I think you would welcome him, tend to his needs, "suck up to him", make available to him anything he required to do the job at hand.

How did this world ever reach the stage where we think Amway is more important than God? Too often, us humans are too slow, proud, arrogant or stupid and think that we are so important. The reality is that we should be seriously "sucking up" to God!

In Old Testament times, people called on God via a human being, a priest. This priest would take the requests to the Tabernacle and pray to God the Father as an intercessor for the people.

In New Testament times, Jesus Christ lived on earth and people were able to learn from him, sit under his teaching and instruction, follow his example and do as he directed them to do. As well as teaching the people that they could take their prayers directly to the Father, he also told them that they would receive the Holy Spirit when Jesus ascended to heaven.

From the Book of Acts until the end of this age, we no longer need a priest and Jesus is not visually standing alongside of us, but we have access to heaven through the Holy Spirit. This is his turn to be our guide. And that is what he wants to do.

No matter how willing we are to do our bit, God *will* reign supreme. He *will* be praised and acknowledged for who he is.

He instructs us and gives us the opportunity to know him so we:
- Recognise him when He reigns;
- Can be a part of his works;
- Are saved when he comes;
- Can see his wonderful works.

I urge you to please keep working on knowing God better, knowing the Bible, his character and his desires for us. As you go through this book, I hope you are learning ways to do that, but now please spend some time with him. Just talk with him, listen to him, share experiences and feel his closeness. Doing this regularly will improve your relationship with him and give you a greater insight into his idea of helping the others that he has, and will, put into your life. There are many good books on prayer if you're struggling in that area, but for now my advice is go and talk to your friend, God! Get to know God.

Key Points:
- The danger is becoming good people who don't do anything that matters;
- The Spirit never guilts you - he guides you;
- God's motives are 100% pure;
- We should be seriously 'sucking up' to God;
- Keep working on knowing God better.

Application for Chapter 4: In God's Hands

1. Recall a time when you felt the power of the Holy Spirit working through you. What most excites you about having the Holy Spirit live in you, working through you? Explain.

   _____

   _____

2. Thank God for three things that you have prayed for, but not yet seen the results. Are you still trusting in faith that you will see the answers?

   _____

   _____

3. Identify two ways you are *willing*, but not yet *able*, to make yourself available for God's work

   _____

   _____

4. Identify two ways you are *able*, but not yet *willing*, to make yourself available for God's work

   _____

   _____

5. Select one Bible reference mentioned in this chapter. Write it out on another piece of paper and put it on your fridge. Memorise it this week. Now, write it here in your own words.

   _____

   _____

   _____

   _____

6. What areas do you need to work on to be more usable in God's hands?

   _____

   _____

   _____

   _____

7. Spend some time talking to God in the manner he deserves - with some major "sucking up". Feel free to make any notes here that resulted from that prayer time.

   _____

   _____

   _____

   _____

108

Salvation THROUGH...

Chapter 5: You're a Tool

You are worth much more than any inanimate object tossed in the back of a work van. You are also a lot more versatile. In God's hands, you are a tool that he wants to use to work his wonders here on his earth. Let's open your toolkit and take a look, before doing a restock of it.

We are all a part of his toolkit

Look at 1 Corinthians 12:27-28. "Now you are the body of Christ, and each one of you is a part of it. And in the church God has appointed first of all apostles, second prophets, third teachers, then workers of miracles, also those having gifts of healing, those able to help others, those with gifts of administration, and those speaking in different kinds of tongues."

The word 'help' used here is the word 'boetheia' (bo-ay-thi-ah) meaning 'to aid'; specifically, a rope or chain for frapping a vessel. If you are like me and have to check the dictionary for words like 'frapping', here's what I found. The word 'frap' is defined as "Bind tightly". That's quite a strong type of help. God's idea of help isn't cotton holding paper; He has given the gift of help strong enough to tie a vessel together and tightly!

Okay, so not everyone gets a gift, right? Wrong. Read verse 28 again, "each of you is a part of it." God gives gifts to *all* his children; some just *choose* not to accept them or use them. Would you deliberately leave one of your gifts under the Christmas tree? I wouldn't. We are *all* part of the *one* body and therefore we should all fit together and use all the skills he gave.

As one body, we should also know how the body works. It is important not to try to be all to all. Rather, be wise enough and in-tune enough, to know when to refer a job to others. Have you considered Romans 8:11, 'And if the Spirit of him who raised Jesus from the dead is living in you, he who raised Christ from the dead will also give life to your mortal bodies through his spirit, who lives in you.'

He does not expect us to do it all alone. Can you imagine him saying to a parent, "raise this child on your own, accept no help from family, friends, teachers, neighbours, or anyone? Use no tools, no shelter or clothing, nothing that has been created. Do this totally solo." No, God knows the benefits of assisting others, in sharing resources, in providing for the needs of others. Remember too, he has given every one of us different skills and gifts, so who are we to think we could possess all of them? Granted, some people seem to be a lot more capable of a lot more than some other people, but we all have something different to offer.

In 1 Corinthians 10:13 we are reminded that "God is faithful; He will not let you be tempted beyond what you can bear. But when you are tempted, He will also provide a way out so that you can stand up under it." Put simply, he will not allow us to go through anything that, together, he and we cannot handle. While this verse is mainly talking about temptation, it also applies to the ability to cope in any situation. In fact, when faced with the option of helping a friend in need, you may be tempted to ignore it, palm them off to someone else, or even to "help" them by doing the task for them (this is not always the best way to help, but we'll look at that later). God knows what he wants you to do in that situation. Your job is to listen to him.

In short, take comfort in knowing that God will give you whatever information, tool, time, money, ideas, manpower – *anything* - that is necessary to help someone that he wants you to help. He does not promise to help you to fulfil all *your* ideas for helping people. As I said in the introduction, and as we will learn later, the key to being God's Helper is knowing God, it is *not* about just doing or being busy.

It's a pretty good deal to get three for one. God the Father wants to help. Jesus wants to help. The Holy Spirit wants to help. If you went to a foreign country, you may need to use an interpreter or other type of different resource to achieve your goals while you weren't able to communicate fully. Similarly, each person of the trinity has a different form and function, so they decided to use us as resources, to use our fingers and toes. The fingers and toes that *they* made, the gifts / digits that *they* chose for *you*. Jesus was a carpenter and we are his tools. God created the world with his voice and we're his modern tools.

God has given us all the tools to do the job HE wants us to do

Too often we decide to do our own thing. Consider the outcome if God gave me the tool to be a carpenter and I decided that I was going to be a cook. No matter how much I ask him to help me be a great cook, if that is not his will for me, the tools won't work. What good is the saw going to be for cooking a soufflé? How is the electric drill going to marinade the chicken? And wouldn't the screws taste terrible in the salad! We need to be doing his will, not ours. And only he knows each tool needed for each project and who, where, when and how to implement the job.

When we are doing the right thing, in the right place, at the right time, we tend to be a spiritual example! Ephesians 6:14-16 instructs us to put on the: "Belt of truth buckled around your waist, with the breastplate of righteousness in place, and with your feet fitted with the readiness that comes from the gospel of peace ... take up the shield of faith *with which you can extinguish all the flaming arrows of the evil one* ... the helmet of salvation and the sword of Spirit, which is the word of God." This verse is usually referred to in reference to spiritual battles. I think it should be our daily lifestyle.

Psalm 108:12 says, "Give us aid against the enemy, for the help of man is worthless." Here the word 'help' is teshuwah (tesh-oo-ah) which means rescue (lit or fig, pers, national or spir); deliverance, help, safety, salvation, victory. And, as is so often the case in the Bible, the Old Testament works with the New Testament.

How do we apply Ephesians 6:14-16 to what God instructed us in Psalm 108:12? We apply the tools he gave us. So, let's combine the key words from the Psalm with those from the passage in Ephesians.

God please give us aid (tools such as: truth, righteousness, preparation and peace, faith, salvation, word of God) when we are faced with the enemy (something that is not of God, is dangerous or disruptive), because the type of help that man offers (deliverance, help, safety, salvation, victory) is worthless.

In the Psalm, David is asking God for help against the enemy. Many times, we take the lazy way out, telling ourselves, "there's nothing I can do. This is a 'spiritual battle' so the situation or person needs God not me".

What we need to remember is that we, yes we mere human beings with all our shortcomings, are the help - the aid - that God uses to help his people in times of spiritual attacks. The help of man is worthless if it is directed by man. But, when we are used by God, with the power of God and all his tools flowing through us, the mere human becomes powerful!

Key Points:
- God's idea of help is strong and powerful;
- We all have gifts from God;
- God has access to every tool he needs; be the one he chooses;
- God promises to give you every resource to fulfil his plan, not yours;
- We need to use the tools he gave us for their intended purpose.

You're the one on ground level

In the gospel of Matthew, we see several examples of helping, shown to us by the Lord Jesus himself. Let's look at chapter 9 verses 35-37.

In verse 35, "Jesus went through all the towns and villages, teaching in their synagogues, preaching the good news of the kingdom and healing every disease and sickness." What will your project be? Teaching, preaching, performing miracles of faith (helping the diseased), or practical help (helping the sick)? Do you have a particular aptitude, compassion, calling towards any of these, or any other way of helping people?

In verse 36 we see that "When He [Jesus] saw the crowds, He had compassion on them, because they were harassed and helpless, like sheep without a shepherd." Are you compassionate? Do you see under people's masks and see when they are feeling harassed or helpless? Do you see the needs in other people's lives and have a burden to help? Don't lose that, let's just try to channel it so that we get it right, and the only way to get something right is to let God be the boss of it.

Then, in verse 37, Jesus said to His disciples, "the harvest is plentiful, but the workers are few. Ask the Lord of the harvest, therefore, to send out workers into his harvest field."

In the workplace, if you are stressed and over-burdened, you have the right to take that need to the boss and ask for assistance. That assistance may come in the form of another staff member or even a faster computer. Most *good* business owners are not going to deny the request if your motive is right, because they are even more interested in having their business succeed than you are.

And they know if you're not getting through your workload because you are lazy. If that's the case, they won't spend more money to 'help' you. That wouldn't be helping you to get your job done. That would be a *bad help*. But if your request is genuine, they will honour it because they appreciate having staff on hand who are as keen as they are to meet the goals of their business.

They also know that you have an additional level of knowledge because you are on the ground level. You have access to the customers, conveyor belts, records or whatever the job entails. In the world of Workplace Health & Safety, consultation is so important that it has a place in the Acts, Regulations and Standards. The expectations are so high that there are consultation courses, programs and policies to ensure it is implemented in the workplace.

How much more so does God understand the need to have his business, the business of salvation, succeed? He wants to reach every market in the globe and he, too, needs you because you are on the ground level. So, go to God with the request that he give you more workers and he *will* grant your request.

Sadly though, just as not everyone will accept Jesus as saviour, not everyone will accept the challenge asked by God to work in his fields. But, it is one of our responsibilities to ask him for more workers, to have a diligent interest in the Business of God here on earth.

Just prior to reading the above Matthew verses, I asked God whether this book was just for me or is this lesson to become a publication for others to read and learn.

God would like us *all* to do what he's teaching here, but the sad reality is that *few* will. Therefore, like today's pyramid selling schemes, we need to recruit others who in turn will engage other workers so that (and this is the result) the one at the top gets all the glory and honour. Truthfully though, in the world's pyramid selling, the one at the top doesn't deserve credit (or money) any more than the one at the bottom. With God, however, the one at the top deserves every iota of credit, honour, glory and praise that we could ever possibly give him - and then more.

So, here is this book, a job description for all of those in God's kingdom to see who will apply for one of the many positions available as Helpers of the Lord.

God prepares people to do what is required for him to answer the prayers of others. We see examples of this in the book of Acts where God used Ananias in Saul's conversion.

In Acts 9:10-12, the Lord called to Ananias in a vision, "Go to ... Saul, for he is praying. In a vision he has seen a man name Ananias come and place his hands on him to restore his sight." Of course, he goes, and in verse 18 we are told, "Immediately, something like scales fell from Saul's eyes, and he could see again".

Ananias was scared, but obedient to God's instructions and purpose. God shared with Ananias in verse 15 that Saul "is my chosen instrument to carry my name..."

God had a plan. He chose the tool, Ananias, to help Saul so that Ananias would be blessed, Saul would praise God, and multitudes would become eternally saved.

As we saw in the Help-Save Cycle, God selects the *tool* for this situation (a miraculous storm or a helper) and then God, through the helper / tool, provides the *help* (teaching, food, prayer).

We know that he firstly selects the right *tool* for this given situation and uses that tool to provide the answer to the need at hand.

You're a tool. You're the one that is here on the ground - the connection between God and his people. Sometimes you may be a hose and sometimes you may be a teaspoon or a measuring cup. But if you allow God to work through you then you will be the right tool for the best outcome for the person he is helping at that time.

Ecclesiastes 4:10 tells us, "If one falls down, his friend can help him up. But pity the man who falls and has no one to help him up!"

We can't prevent people falling, even if we are a friend or are right there beside them. In the physical world, there are things we cannot prevent. We also each need to go through the lessons of falling, to learn all that is gained from these experiences. What we can do is try to make sure everyone has someone to depend on, to help them up. Someone to help when they are down, and when they are getting up, and when they are on their feet. Don't assume, don't use human logic to decide someone has had enough help. Be there until God says his work is done.

In rural NSW there is a small campground. Julie and Bruce have been there a few times and became friends with the owner. Following a prompting by the Holy Spirit, Bruce said to Julie, "Do you mind if I go to the café for a while?" Having no objection, he wandered across the paddock to the café.

Here Bruce said to the café owner, "Would you mind if I help out a bit and clean up for a while? It's so hot and you've been so busy, so I'd like to help." The café owner cried. Bruce spent the next two hours wiping tables, hosing paths, emptying garbage bins and generally cleaning up.

Julie went over a while later and sat at one of the tables, mainly because she loves being with her husband. With the air of hospitality that she emits, two guests assumed she worked there. One asked about staying overnight and the other returned a necklace she found there. Julie said, "I don't work here but I'll take it straight to the staff." Now that's trust.

When they had finished, the owner told Bruce, "Thank you. Now the staff will be able to get home on time tonight." But the reason God knew this woman needed help and had Bruce and Julie step in, was in what she said next. She confided, "We've been so overwhelmed here and we're down a person. My husband died a few weeks ago".

There is no way Bruce could have known that. He had no motive to help, just the prompting of the Spirit of God. And there was no way this woman would have asked a guest to help clean, especially without paying them, but God saw her need and responded.

We may never know, and don't need to know, the reasons or the big picture. We don't need to know if she was crying the night before, asking God for help. It is none of our business. That's between her and God.

Furthermore, we are not omnipresent. We can fool others but only God knows our heart, so it would be audacious to think that we could know what another person wanted or needed, what was good or bad for them in any given situation, or what they were thinking. Heck, we misinterpret what people say out loud!

Let's just take a moment to praise God, because in this situation:
- Bruce was able to hear God's prompting;
- Bruce followed the prompt and put it into action. Humbly;
- Julie was an example of God, one that others saw, a witness;
- The staff were cared for with an early finish;
- The owner's practical and personal needs were met.

Key Points:
- You're the one here on the ground - the connection between God and his people;
- Do you have a particular aptitude, calling, compassion? Channel it;
- God wants his business of salvation to grow, so he will provide the leads;
- Opposite to pyramid schemes, God at the top deserves all the glory;
- We don't need to know, nor are we capable of knowing, all the details.

Accepting the mission

We all know the story about Jonah. God gave him a job, he refused and rebelled, and a huge fish swallowed him whole. But the story doesn't end there. In fact, that is the part of the story that we can all identify with! The reason the story is in the Bible is for us to learn a lesson from what happened next.

"From inside the fish Jonah prayed to the Lord his God. He said: 'In my distress I called to the Lord, and He answered me'." (Jonah 2:1-2)

Jonah finally realised the error of his ways and repented. Because of this repentance and cry for help, God allowed the fish to save Jonah - physically. He actually *used* this creature, as he uses people, to be instruments (tools) in the process to help us get where he wants us to be. I mean, the fish could have chewed Jonah up into bits, and if God weren't in control, I'm sure it would have. In fact, engulfed in all that bile and smell, I think Jonah probably wished it had. Lessons aren't meant to be pleasant.

You see, God knows in advance how we will react to every test and trial he allows us to go through. It's just that we are so slow to learn that he is forced to give us many tests until we truly grasp what it is that we need to learn. This lesson is always beneficial to us, so I still don't understand why we struggle for so long. Remember, that God is always more interested in our best interests than we are.

So, what was the result of Jonah's trial? He re-prioritised his life, gave thanks to God, did the job God asked him to do in the first place, and recalled the purpose of salvation.

Then in Jonah 2:8-9 we read, "Those who cling to worthless idols forfeit the grace that could be theirs. But I, with a song of thanksgiving, will sacrifice to you. What I have vowed I will make good. Salvation comes from the Lord."

God heard his servant's cry for help, he provided help and that person praised God. And it didn't stop there. We later read in Matthew 12:41, "The men of Nineveh will stand up at the judgement with this generation and condemn it; for they repented at the preaching of Jonah." I wonder how the men of Nineveh would have become saved if Jonah didn't repent first? I wonder how many others will now spend eternity in heaven because of the preaching and teaching of those men and their families.

Jonah did his part, though a little late, so that others would receive salvation. What a lot of wasted lives there would have been if Jonah hadn't repented and was eaten by the big fish.

This gives us a little insight into the repercussions (both good and bad) of our actions. In this case, Jonah's disobedience led to his obedience which led to people being saved. Nearly a thousand years later in New Testament times, and through to today where the lesson of the story is still being taught, Jonah's experience is being used as a tool to get people into heaven. *God does not just use good things, he also takes our struggles, our disobedience, our shortcomings to use for his purpose.* What is that purpose? To bless man and glorify God.

Isaiah 41:28 reveals, "I look but there is no one - no one among them to give counsel, no one to give answer when I ask them." God asks people, leaders and even idols, to prove themselves but they can't (of course). "He saw that there was no one, he was appalled that there was no one to intercede; so his own arm worked salvation for him, and his own righteousness sustained him" (Isaiah 59:16).

God doesn't expect us to all be apostles, leaving our day job and our families and following him. His request is to be available and in the right place, so that he can do his work. God wants to accomplish things in this world, and he will not leave those things undone. We all have a choice. Will we join him in accomplishing His purpose?

I need to point out that, as important as you are in this work, you are only *a* tool, not *the* one and only tool. If you don't accept the job or do it in his time, he will find someone else. His love for his people is that strong.

In saying that, please consider this for a moment.

Are you anxiously longing for the return of Jesus and the commencement of our eternal lives in heaven?

God told us that he will not end the world as we know it until everyone has had the opportunity to choose heaven or hell. So,

God cannot go against his word, so he cannot come back until everyone has had the chance to know him. This usually starts with knowing about him. No, I am not talking about witnessing.

If you want Jesus to return soon, then the responsibility is on us to do our role in sharing God to the world. Reveal God's character of loving, helping others and helping his people love others and serve others in doing so. So yes, he will move on and find someone else to do the job, but we are slowing down the process by not doing our part.

My salvation came as a miracle. I agree that every life saved is a miracle and I know that God can bring salvation in any way that he chooses, but mine did not seem to require any conscious effort on my part at all.

In my eighth month of my first pregnancy, my wardrobe was unintentionally simple - dresses for going out and pants for wearing around the home. My mother had started going to a new church and was getting a lift each week with Aunty Sue. I was not at all interested, often telling her that, "church is for *those* type of people."

On Sunday 22nd September 1985 I woke as if in a daze, put on a dress and rang Sue to see if she had room to pick me up too. I wanted to go to church. I don't recall the sermon, but at the end I responded to the altar call and committed my life to God. At that point, my life became saved and I was born again.

The ease of my salvation has caused me much frustration over the years. I have seen people that have been important to me refuse to come to the Lord. I have prayed many times "Lord, you intervened and saved me, so I know you can do it. Why won't you just save that person? It is your will that everyone be saved. It would be good for them and for your kingdom. Why won't you?"

While that is all true, unfortunately, there are humans involved. It may be that there is a testimony or a gift that God knows will be the turning point for those people, but the tool he has chosen for the task hasn't done their job yet. What an awesome responsibility that puts on us, to do what he wants when he wants. Only God knows the perfect timing for each person's salvation. He always does his part at the perfect time. The question is, do we?

"The Lord had seen how bitterly everyone in Israel, whether slave or free, was suffering; there was no one to help them. And since the Lord had not said he would blot out the name of Israel from under heaven, he saved them by the hand of Jeroboam son of Jehoash." (2 Kings 14:26-27)

God had an obligation. He was not against Israel and therefore he was for them. Note there was no one to help them, yet God saved them by the hand of Jeroboam. Does this mean that Jeroboam was a helper? Yes and no. God used him as one of his tools to help others, so yes, he was a helper. But not technically. *God is looking for people that say, "Here I am Lord, use me"*. He wants people who live their lives for him, his way and under his direction and instruction. Jeroboam wasn't available, so no. But, if in any precise place and time there is none of them to be found (how sad is that!) then he has the awesome power to select and use any tool he wants to - human or otherwise. Wouldn't it be better if he had a selection of helpers to choose from at any place and any time? Let's be available to help God, not because he - great and marvellous God that he is - needs our help, but because that is his first preference, to use *the tools that he created* for the job that he wants done in the way that he wants it done.

Key Points:
- Lessons aren't meant to be pleasant;
- God doesn't just use perfect things;
- You are a tool, not the one and only tool;
- God knows the steps each person will take to their salvation;
- God is looking for people that say, "Here I am Lord, use me".

Your Toolkit

So, God in His wisdom, has decided that we make very useful tools. He wants us to be available so that when he decides to bless someone, he has access to the hands and feet that make the task happen.

In 1 Corinthians 12:12-26 Paul likens the body of Christ, the church, to human body parts. To take this one step further, we could say that this human body is one of the Holy Spirit's toolkits.

So, consider your whole being is your toolkit. What's in yours? Look deeper inside the toolbox. Your experiences. Your knowledge. Your skills. Your personality. Your contacts.

I possess a toolkit. In it are things like:
- Hands to drive, carry, deliver;
- Feet to run, exercise, transport my other tools;
- Eyes to see the world around me and into the eyes of others;
- Brain to learn, decide, understand;
- Experiences to enable empathy for others and the skills to apply them;
- Relationships to draw on.

It is important to acknowledge that this toolkit is:
- Owned by God - He is my creator;
- Operated by the Holy Spirit - he is my guide, and does the works;
- Managed by me – this is the part that can let the team down as I make decisions based on my limited knowledge, my moods, my interpretation of my abilities, my health and so forth.

When my kids were entering their teenage years, one of the slang insults of the day was to call someone a "tool". It implied that you had the brains of an inanimate object, cannot do anything substantial and were disposable.

At this time, God was teaching me that we are to be available for his use. The more I trust in him, the less I trust in myself, the more we work together, the better my life works. Despite my children's mockery, I am proud to be a tool. I long to be a tool. "Please Lord, you control my life! Whenever I take control, I muck it up. Please, please *you* be the one who directs my every move. Use me to do what you intend for me to do and don't let me do anything on my own."

I want to be an object used wholly and solely for God's intended purpose, in his hands, under his direction. God, make me a tool! My prayer was God please *bend me, break me, mould me, make me*. The insult phased out, but today I still beg, "Lord, please make me a tool".

Take Me, **by Mearle Mason**

> *Take my eyes Lord and look through me*
> *Search for the lost sheep I cannot see.*
> *Take my lips Lord and speak through me*
> *The Word that's needed to set men free.*
> *Take my hands Lord and touch through me*
> *The sick and broken who need but Thee.*
> *Take my feet Lord, walk where you will*
> *But find the lost ones who need Thee still.*
> *Take my ears Lord and help me hear*
> *The cries and the sighs of those in despair.*
> *Take my whole being and use me Lord*
> *To bring Thee glory Loved Son of God.*
> *Break me and mould me if that has to be*
> *SO that others can see Christ living in me.*

The Shell for God to work through

As we have seen, God wants to live his life on earth by selecting bodies to work through. He selects mouths to speak to people, he selects hands to write letters of encouragement and to do the manual labour of help. In short, the Holy Spirit selects us to be the shell that he can work through. For this, he needs us to be available and the only way for us to be available is to know him in a personal way. Not just knowing about him and his plan for everyone but knowing him and his plan for me, the person reading this.

Paul told us in Ephesians 2:10 "For we are God's workmanship, created in Christ Jesus to do good works, which God prepared in advance for us to do." God's way - the best way, the perfect way - is for Him to use us to be the shell that He works through.

This is what God wants with us, a relationship where the lines of communication are always open. He doesn't just want us to call on him when we are desperate. But, by being available when we are desperate, he shows his willingness to help us and to be a part of our lives. He reaffirms his desire for a deeper relationship. In this way, we learn to talk to him when we're not desperate and our relationship gets even closer.

One of the great results of knowing someone well is that, when things go wrong, they understand and genuinely care about you. They don't step back in judgement.

What better tool to have on our side than being able to know how God would solve a problem? Can you imagine having that at work? In maths class? In your marriage? When choosing a career path?

Can you represent his desires?

It has always been a pleasure to watch my sister and her husband, particularly their love and devotion to each other. There is no doubt in the mind of anyone that knows them that they just live for each other (and God, but here I am referring to their marital relationship).

They spend every available moment with each other. They are each other's best friend and always have been. They talk about anything, and confide in each other about everything. They do most things together. They simply long to be together.

They know each other so well that, when they are apart, either one can answer questions on the other's behalf. If one was in the bathroom, the other could order their meal for them because they know the likes and dislikes of the other so well. If someone needed help, each one knows how the other would assist in providing that help. If one was asked if the other would be interested in participating in … (a new group, a meeting, a job, anything) they know the other so intimately that they could confidently answer on their behalf.

Here are some thoughts to ponder before doing the application questions:

How's your relationship with God? Do you know him so intimately that you could confidently answer on his behalf? Can you answer questions in the same way he would? Do you know what jobs he wants done and in what order? Do you know how he feels and reacts when he sees someone in need? Can you truly represent God in his (physical) absence?

Key Points:
- What's in your toolkit?
- The more I trust God, the less I trust myself;
- The more we work together, the better my life works;
- God please: Bend me. Break me. Mould me. Make me;
- Be the shell for God to work through.

Application for Chapter 5: You're a Tool

1. Why does God use people to help with his work?

   _____
   _____

2. In what ways has God used you directly? What areas of your life have you handed over to God saying, "God use me, I am just a tool, ready and willing to be used by you whenever you want?" In what ways are you taking control of your life?

   _____
   _____
   _____
   _____

3. Thinking of yourself as a toolbox. Write a list of tools that you possess (eg good eyes, building experience, talents…) and beside each, write a way the Holy Spirit could use this

   _____
   _____
   _____
   _____

4. How have you applied this in the past?) What have you used these tools for in the past? Ie how do you spend your time?

_____
_____

5. Select one Bible reference mentioned in this chapter. Write it out on another piece of paper and put it on your fridge. Memorise it this week. What does this verse mean to you personally?

_____
_____

6. Name 3 ways you are not perfect. Beside each, write why that does not matter in God's toolkit.

_____
_____

7. Spend some time with God, starting with, "Here I am Lord, use me…" Feel free to make any notes here that resulted from that prayer time.

_____
_____

Salvation THROUGH...

Chapter 6: Preparing Yourself for the Job

Being ready for God to work through is not about making your life perfect. None of us can be perfect, so why put that pressure on ourselves, or on others. It is about being available. It means preparing your *heart, mind, words* and *deeds* so that the Holy Spirit can easily work through you. You need to be so at-one with God that you can hear him when he speaks.

Applying for the job

Imagine this: You've seen an advertisement for a job, and it sparks an interest somewhere inside you. You wonder about the role itself, the company, the culture, the pay, the hours and whether you are suitable.

This job is a Labour Hire, 'Temp' position, as in you are employed by one company but working on location on another worksite. So, you need to know the employer company who is paying you, their rules and standards. You also need to know the daily operations of the worksite where you will be doing your job. You need to know their policies, plans, culture, layout, demographics and personalities of all involved. Depending on the role you play, over time you will learn about the problems and requirements of the customers and the interactions between all personnel involved. You will offer solutions to problems and you will get to know people on a more intimate basis, though strictly professional of course.

One of the most important aspects to understand about this job is believing that God knows your innermost thoughts and motivations and sees everything you do. More so, he still loves you and wants to work with you, because you are a unique combination of every thought, action and experience. No other human being in history, now, or in the future will have the exact same life experience as you. There will be similarities, but it is the combination of events and responses that make you who and what you are.

God uses this uniqueness when preparing you to meet and help other people. He uses it when deciding where to best place you for your next assignment. He uses it to make you stronger, help others, and give him the glory.

God is the employer, you are the employee

When we think God's not doing his job and we're losing the battle, we need to trust that, "in all things God works for the good of those who love him" (Romans 8:28).

One problem with us trying to plan everything is that we simply cannot know every detail. Unlike God. In Deuteronomy 7:22 when Moses was talking to the Israelites about eliminating their enemies, he told them, "The Lord your God will drive out those nations before you, little by little. You will not be allowed to eliminate them all at once, or the wild animals will multiply around you."

God made the earth we live on. He knows the order of things. He understands the food chain more than we ever could. From this situation we can learn that:

- He is maintaining the natural food chain, or else they'd all die! He hasn't simply created a bunch of random animals and let them roam around free. He knows the precise number of every type of being;
- He has perfect timing; he does not succumb to the pressures of war or hierarchy;
- He has a plan and a purpose; he alone knows the humanly

unforeseeable future and how every atom works together;

- We should not be greedy or self-focused; too often we are short-sighted and only think of the immediate dangers. We need to trust that God knows more than us;

- Don't be impatient, there is often a reason why things have to occur *"little by little"*.

Good is from God, not you. I have been using the same Chocolate Slice recipe since I was about eight. My mother used it, and so did her mother. The exact same recipe has been made thousands of time by members of my family. Yet, in recent years, something is different. The steps haven't changed, the quantity of each of the ingredients hasn't changed. So, what has?

Eggs could have changed from what they were 50 years ago. Chooks eat different grains, which have changed as a result of changing soil and fertiliser levels. Flour changes for the same reason. Acid rain, humidity, flood and drought all have an impact on our crops which, ever so slightly, vary the resulting food supply.

What about other changes like moving from imperial to metric? The size of the slice tin has changed, altering the height of the slice, thereby changing the way the heat is distributed. Milk is another source that has changed considerably over the years.

Now, all of these will only produce miniscule alterations, but can you see how even the smallest of changes can have an effect on the outcome. These results may be for better or worse, or they may just be different, and not alter the taste at all.

Even more than changing eggs, no two humans are ever identical. All the combinations and variables in every aspect make us different, just like in the ingredients in a slice.

Why am I telling you this? Because our contribution to helping another person will vary every time. Don't assume that you can help one person exactly the same as another and get exactly the same result. Outwardly, factors may look similar, but there will be different results on the inner person.

And remember that your ingredients may have a positive, negative, or neutral effect on others. So, make sure you are in the hands of the great chef and allow him to put the best ingredients in the right mixture at the right time. Allow him to be the employer and you maintain your role of employee.

Before applying for this job, that of helper not chef, you need to accept that God alone knows your true inner being, and that of everyone else you will have contact with. Be willing to let him use that knowledge for his plan. You won't always see the results. It won't always make sense, but trust that God is in control and has a much greater interest in your daily life than you ever will.

I am going to show you a job description. I want you to read it and think about it. Is this the job for you? Would you apply for this job? Does it look like a lot of work? Are you wondering whether you would be suitable?

Unlike the human world we live in, even when we doubt our ability, God already knows that you are right for this job. If you decide that you want the job, your next step is usually to sit down and write your application.

In Australia, applying for a job can be a very big task. Depending on the type of job, you might need to write a Cover Page. This outlines why you are the best person for the position, while telling more about yourself that your resume doesn't cover. Then, there's the Selection Criteria that must be addressed. There are usually between six and twenty questions and you have to write a paragraph on each. Then, of course, your Resume. This is the documented history of your working life - all the roles you've had, the companies you've worked for, the duration of each and your achievements along the way.

And each of these three documents are competing with every other applicant for the same job, before the employer ever meets you. If you make it through to the Short List, you will be required to attend at least one interview, and possibly practical or aptitude tests to verify your suitability.

No matter what the job, the application process, is very daunting and time consuming. However, all of this is quiclyly forgotten once you are successful and working in the role. Another good thing about working in God's kingdom is that we don't have to write an application. God knows our heart, and there are jobs for as many people as want them.

"For you alone know the hearts of all men." (1 Kings 8:39b)

"God, who knows the heart..." (Acts 15:8)

"...but God knows your hearts..." (Luke 16:15b)

Let's take a look at your job description.

Be the shell of HELP through which salvation comes
POSITION AVAILABLE: God's Helper

Job Description:
God requires helpers through which he can provide the necessary tools to lead Christians to repentance and non-Christians to salvation.

Skills Required:

Flexibility	- to be able to change your plans as the employer allocates his projects
Armour	- to be fully equipped with the protective equipment supplied by the employer
Teachable	- to be willing to learn from those above you
Humility	- to put aside your own desires and ideas, accepting whole-heartedly your employer's directions
Eagerness	- keen to work, learn and help
Real	- be a living example of Jesus; God sees through falsity
Geography	- a good sense of direction so you are able to seek and find God at any time
Organised	- able to balance your family, career and this job
Dreamer	- dare to believe in miracles

Experience Required:
1. Good communication skills - A strong prayer experience is an advantage
2. Bad track record is an advantage - Any negative life experience is beneficial as the Master turns it into empathy

Duties:
To assist / aid / help in meeting the needs of others as determined by the Master

Some examples of projects performed by previous employees

Practical	Personal	Spiritual
· help with heavy loads · employ others to give them a financial start · provide food, drink, clothing, shelter · teach · lend or sell at no profit	· uplift after a fall · visit the sick · visit the imprisoned · encourage · care for the sick	· live in his will · perform miracles · pray for workers · pray for needy · strengthen others' faith

Bonuses:
Often paid immediately - seeing the results of your role in causing others to do something that brings about changes in their lives, now and eternally

Hours:
On-call 24/7 but individual tasks will be determined by the employer on a case-by-case basis

Wages:
All the tools, knowledge, skills, directions and wisdom are provided by the employer and are yours to keep after each project
Daily payments of joy and satisfaction
Long Service Leave entitlements at the end of your term
Retirement payments are invested into a SuperB Fund - paid into your Heavenly Retirement Fund

To Apply:
Seek Management and speak to them directly, acknowledging to them all of your strengths and abilities, then submit yourself to them.

Key Points:

- No other human being in history, now, or in the future will have the exact same life experience as you;
- We cannot follow the exact steps and assume the exact outcome with people - we're all unique;
- Make sure you are in the hands of the "Great Chef" and allow him to put the best ingredients in;
- Are you ready to apply for the job?
- Good is from God, not you.

Stop being busy

So, you applied for a job, were successful, and you start work in one week. What now? Now you need to prepare yourself for the job.

Your home life probably needs a bit of adjusting. If you haven't been working and have children, you may need to find a child-carer. You may want to give your home a spring clean, knowing you will soon have less time, and will be tired until you settle into your new routine. You will possibly need to buy, or iron, some suitable clothes. So, in the time leading up to your new start, spend some time preparing yourself for this job.

Prepare your:	When starting to work for a human boss you:	When starting to work for God you:
Time	Organise your diary or calendar	Stop being busy
House	Have a spring clean	Give over the reins
Knowledge	Research both companies and clientele	Strengthen your mind to be able to hear and know his plans
Uniform	Prepare your clothing	Prepare your armour
Toolkit	Source tools, set the alarm	Prepare your tools for work
Mind	Be willing to learn from the very beginning	Stop thinking like a human
Position	Identify your role, humbly	Ask: where do I, as a human, fit it?

The key to being God's Helper is knowing him. It is *not* about just doing or being busy.

My mother came from London and so was very familiar with snow. During a particularly cold Australian winter, I asked if she thought it could snow. She told me that, "it's too cold to snow." As a child, I thought that snow was the result of extreme coldness, so her answer didn't initially compute to my way of thinking. Just like it can be too cold to produce cold outcomes, we can be too busy to produce anything helpful. The truth is that you can be *too* qualified for a job, a fruit can be *too* ripe to eat, it can be *too* cold to snow, and you can be *too* busy to do anything helpful. Being a helper is not about being industrious. Like the weather can be too extreme to perform the obvious, you can be too busy to be of any use to God at all!

Helper tip: It's very important for all parties that the helper allows other people to help them too. Don't think you have to do everything alone.

Now I am not suggesting you simply sit and twiddle your thumbs while waiting for an assignment, what boss wants that? It's not good for your physical or mental health either, and being a part of the daily grind gives you more knowledge and experience with your work. You learn the tricks of the trade by doing something repetitively.

Being available means being flexible. It means spending your time doing things that can be modified, postponed or put on hold when your employer calls you up with an assignment. Spend your time doing things that interact with his calling. No, do not quit your current job! You may just need to change employers! To achieve this, you may need to *change your work-sight rather than your work-site*. You can change the way you see your workplace, your role, and your priorities.

You need to remember that God is your employer, he gives your appointments, all the resources and he pays your wages. So, when you're at work, and he calls, how do you respond?

Get rid of the busy-ness that your plans have created. Become the shell that he can work through. Live in God's will and be able to jump when he calls. Sometimes, we have to cleanse our diaries to open time for other things.

The tool in God's hands doesn't have to be as profound and decisive as the toolbox, but it has to be there and in working condition for him to pick it up and put it to use.

My current morning routine combines a walk with a Gloria Jean's coffee. It's my half hour of thinking, praying and enjoying the elements before I start the day.

One morning I passed a lady who said, "That makes me happy."

Slightly confused, I looked at my mug and she added, "I was wondering if they were open."

My prayer had been, "Good morning God. I know what I think I would like to do today but all of it is open to change. What would you like to add, take away or change?"

Of course, his reply made perfect sense after meeting the coffee lady.

He said, "Just do what you're doing, and I'll be there to make people happy." He didn't need me to stop my non-spiritual coffee walk routine. He wants to be a part of my life and just wants me willing to share it with him. You could think of yourself as a company logo on a moving vehicle. Rather than waiting for the customers to go to the business, the business actively reminds potential customers what's available.

Spiritual maturity

"Brothers, if someone is caught in a sin, you who are spiritual should restore him gently. But watch yourself, or you also may be tempted" (Galatians 6:1).

In responsibilities such as this, it is very important to be spiritually mature before trying to help another person. Maturity doesn't mean being the best, an expert, or even qualified. It means being confident enough to admit you don't know everything, and then being open to listening and learning.

So, it is wise to prepare yourself for the job before you apply so that you are not tempted by the actions of others when you're involved in helping. A long time ago, when I was a very new Christian, a friend and I used to street witness to those in and around pubs. We would have done more harm than good if we had succumbed and joined them in getting drunk. We know that

God can use the incapable and the immature, we cannot limit his abilities. And there are so many examples where he used the least qualified person for a job. However, it is not worth putting your salvation, your relationship with God, his reputation, or the lives of others at risk, just by being content with "God can use anything".

Usually employers are looking for new employees with the *most* experience, but not always. Oftentimes, employers want to employ people with *no* experience in their field so that they don't have to un-train any bad habits that may have been learnt. Always, employers are looking to employee the person who is *most trainable* to their way of thinking and working.

God, too, will employ those who are most trainable, because we aren't of much use when we go off and do what *we* think he wants done *our* way. Remember, only he knows all the circumstances and reasons for the work he wants done.

Have I made you feel guilty yet? You're not alone. I do that to myself too. I have lost count of the number of times that this body should have, literally, died and God has saved it. Yet, *still* I waste time on things of little importance. The message to myself is, 'stop wasting time and get on with God's will!"

It's not hard. Basically, God tells us to think of others and do what is necessary for them rather than what is wanted for ourselves. He will look after our needs. We were told in Jude 22-23 to, "be merciful to those who doubt; snatch others from the fire and save them; to others show mercy, mixed with fear."

Don't panic, you won't always be asked to walk through fire, most acts of helping are quite tame and safe compared to that. He simply wants us to show up, with the Spirit's guidance, and do whatever is necessary. Sometimes, you will be required to say a few words, sometimes you will have to forego a few hours or days to aide someone. At other times, you may need to totally sacrifice something you want to help the other person come to know God. Whatever the case, the outcome is *always* bigger than the input.

"The blessing of the Lord brings wealth, and he adds no trouble to it." (Proverbs 10:22). As a helper for God, it's never been any trouble to help others, even during the times when I didn't feel very close to him (admit it, we've all had those times). That's because helping is his plan, not mine, and so these actions are directed by him.

Key Points:
- The key to being God's helper is knowing God. It is not about just doing or being busy;
- Being a helper is not about being industrious;
- Allow other people to help you too;
- How do you respond when your boss, God, gives you an assignment?
- Change your work-sight, rather than your work-site.

Give over the reins, you are not your own boss

I spent years begging God to control my life. Now it's evident everywhere that I'm not in control. And I'm complaining. I said to God, "I thought, if you were in control then I would look more like you, not like this complaining me." He told me simply, that I can't look like him while I still look like me.

The message was to stop complaining. I am in training. We are all in training. So, when he takes control of parts of your life, then stand firm and the witness, the victory, will be good! I cannot say it any clearer than in 2 Corinthians 5:11b "What we are is plain to God, and I hope it is also plain to your conscience."

Being available to be a helper with God means being willing to *not* be in control of your life. We all have things that need to be done and we all have things that we want to do. But God also has an agenda and it is wise to check his agenda first before making plans of your own. Have you ever had plans that fail? Everyone has. For example, today you may want to: do the shopping, visit your sister, and start reading that new novel.

Now these are all worthwhile things to do, but how many people are going to heaven as a direct result of what you choose to do today?

Try asking God, "Lord, what do *you* want me to do today?" I think you'll find that he doesn't have a heap of nasty chores for you, and he has provided you with all the tools to do it - (love, patience, kindness ... not to mention the time, air, water, mind and everything else required for the job. In fact, you may be pleasantly surprised to find that his plans will often work with yours. He may want you to visit your sister tomorrow because a friend of hers will be there then and that friend is open to the gospel, or is going through a divorce and needs an extra shoulder or a word from an experienced divorcee.

Don't shy away from asking God for his plans. He loves the fact that we are willing to work his way. He, like any other parent or friend, loves being asked. And, he rewards those who do this.

Using the above agenda, today's plans could go either way:
Your way:
- Do the shopping - the queues are unusually long and slow;

- Visit your sister - drive to her house, she isn't home, call her and arrange to go there later, resulting in twice the amount of time and fuel being used, followed by you being frustrated;

- Read that new novel - you open the book and the phone rings, you get back to the book and the doorbell rings, you get back to the book and lo and be hold, it's time to pick the kids up from school. Where did the day go?!

God's way:

- Do the shopping - the aisles and queues are fast, and your groceries are cheaper than you had hoped. He even throws in friendly faces and someone to befriend, say a kind word to, give some money to or help in some other way;

- Visit your sister – you have a lovely calm time together and witness to her friend;

- Read that new novel - God actually wants us to take time to relax and enjoy life so, after you've done his will, you sit down with a cuppa and enjoy a whole hour of uninterrupted reading time, after which you are so happy you make a beautiful evening for yourself and the family!

I am not implying that God makes everything perfect, just that there's a difference when walking in his will. In fact, it's good for us not to have a perfect life. The point is to share your life with him, don't go it alone.

Mark 14:7 tells us how we can help the poor people anytime because God has given us every resource we need for them. "The poor you will always have with you, and you can help them any time you want." If you need to give someone something, rest assured God has already supplied it.

This passage, in its context, also reminds us of another thing to keep in mind when helping others - don't get caught up in doing the work of the Lord so much that you neglect the Lord of the work. God must be your number one priority, otherwise you are not in a position to help anyone properly and all your effort, though it may *look* good, will be in vain and pointless. This doesn't mean you have to spend two hours in Bible study for every one hour of helping - God's not that legalistic. It means, talk to him even while you're driving to the needee's house, commit the task to him, discuss it with him, ask for his help.

God tests us to strengthen us, just like we do to our bodies in exercise. We push ourselves a little bit further each time. Testing us, and making us wait, helps with our patience in the eleventh-hour scenarios. Many times, I have trusted God fully when I ask him, then after waiting a while and *reminding* him, I start to get a bit impatient. Then, by the eleventh hour, I am doubting either my faith, his love for me, or both. These are the kinds of issues he needs us to work through and strengthen, so that in every situation we can stay strong and faithful. I look forward to that day when my test response is me calmly waiting that 'little bit longer' rather than becoming sad, angry, frustrated and doubtful.

We are a lot like plants in this way. Plants need water to survive, but you shouldn't overwater them. By spoiling them in always providing surface top water, they stop striving to survive, stop looking for water, stop pushing those roots further. They can end up falling over, getting diseases and dying because of their shallow roots. God knows that it is essentially *good* for us to suffer.

Key Points:
- I can't look like God when I still look like me;
- Being available means being willing to not be in control;
- Start your day with, "Lord what do *you* want me to do today?"
- God doesn't necessarily have a heap of nasty chores for you;
- Share your life with God, don't do it alone.

Stop thinking like a human

We can be quick to assume, quick to judge and so quick to put our opinions onto other people. I was taking our dog, Fudge, for a walk and watching his interactions with other animals. One oversized scary-looking dog came towards us and I assumed Fudge would be scared or want to burr up and fight but no, he wasn't interested. Another big scary dog let out a deep bark and, again, I assumed that our dog would be scared or feel the need to respond, but neither. Then we saw a guide dog. These are the least of all scary animals, and Fudge wanted to play. He was very interested, tugging at the lead, begging me to take him closer. Then I realised he wanted to play with him because he knew this one was a good dog. Animals have senses, they pick up these things. They know. He wasn't interested in approaching the bad ones, he wanted to play with the good one. I had put my assumptions on the situation.

I was thinking like a human. You see, on two previously walks, I'd experienced other people's dogs come out of their yards without owners or leads. Both times, their dog came aggressively, and fights started. I have a scar on my left leg that reminds me that, even when I do the right thing by having my dog on a lead, there are others who don't always take responsibility for their animals. The event has stayed with me for years. Even now, whenever I am walking a dog, I flinch and turn away from strange dogs interacting.

I took my experiences and I made decisions based on them. I didn't trust God for his safety and direction. My actions were based totally on my interpretation and experiences as a human, not on God's love and power. When things happen quickly, we make decisions based on our default training. This is why it is so important that we live as if God were physically standing next to us, then our default reaction is to ask for his help.

I learnt a valuable lesson the day my grandson had me heartbroken and speechless.

Archer was three and such a joy to be around. It was time for my visit to end and I gave him a hug and said my goodbyes, finishing with, "I'll be back soon."

His reply completely stunned me when he loudly and firmly said, "No. Don't come back!"

My heart stopped. My little mate didn't want to see me again. What could I have possibly done to hurt him that bad?

Then he added, "Don't come back. Just stay. Don't leave!"

He didn't want me to go!

I had interpreted his words based on my understanding of them, not his intended use of them. To think, if he hadn't completed his message, or if I hadn't still been listening, our relationship may have been permanently damaged.

How often have we misinterpreted information? We need to accept that our understanding of a situation is not always God's interpretation, or the intention of others involved in it. I urge you to be willing to try to see things through other people's eyes or, even when you cannot see their version, be willing to accept that yours may not be correct.

Julie was doubting her role in God's plan. They had committed their move to God, and believed that their role in moving to their current residential area was to help other people. Now, after so many relationships have come to an end, she's saddened and thinks she must not be in God's will.

This kind of doubt can be self-destructive. What Julie needed to realise was that she is in God's will. He placed her there to do a particular job with each individual person, not to become lifelong buddies with all of them. That is his plan and she is a part of that. She was thinking like a human.

Often, people think if relationships are good, they last forever, but that's not necessarily true. Nor is that our role. Jesus didn't become lifelong friends with everyone he came in contact with. Staying in permanent relationship with someone is not always part of the process. In fact, being with you may hinder them from doing, being, calling … whatever they need to do next. Life is full of phases and we need to be in various relationships at different times.

Men build houses. They pick up a saw and start cutting timber. If they just kept cutting every piece of timber in the building project, the house wouldn't be very stable. They need to put the saw down and pick up a hammer. They need to use different tools for different jobs at different times.

The other thing about relationships is that we, like all tools, need maintenance. We need time out, a break from the job, to refresh. This is crucial so that when we are required, we are ready, willing and able.

Don't think logic will win!

Have you ever been deflated and left with the thought, "Well that didn't work so it couldn't have been from God"? I know I have, too many times.

David Meece is a brilliant singer and one of my favourite songs is called, "Things You Never Gave Me". It shares the message of thanking God for the times he said "No". It's a story about God not granting us our desires because he knows better.

How often have we planned things with all the knowledge available to us, only to have it fail? Well, thank you, God, for your intervention!

We tend to look at Abraham as being the perfect hero of faith in the Old Testament, but he wasn't perfect. He too made mistakes. Not once, but twice, he told kings that Sarah was his sister rather than his wife. His reason was selfish - so they wouldn't kill him and take Sarah for themselves. The second time, in Genesis 20:2-6 God saved the king by warning him, "I know you did this with a clear conscience, and so I have kept you from sinning against me."

With God's intervention, by him not allowing our plans to go ahead, better things can happen. In Abraham's case by God intervening, he preserved Abraham's life, Sarah's life, their marriage, the king's life, and taught all listeners about obeying and trusting God.

Let's look closer at a few verses from Isaiah 50:5, 7, 9

"The Sovereign Lord has opened my ears, and I have not been rebellious; I have not drawn back…Because the Sovereign Lord helps me, I will not be disgraced. Therefore, have I set my face like flint, and I know I will not be put to shame … It is the Sovereign Lord who helps me. Who is he that will condemn me? They will all wear out like a garment; the moths will eat them up."

We, like Isaiah, need to acknowledge that it is God, the Sovereign Lord, that helps us. When we learn, it is *he* that teaches us, *he* that opens our ears and *he* that enables us to understand things that others don't. "Then he opened their minds so they could understand the Scriptures." (Luke 24:45).

Isaiah learnt this lesson and did not rebel. It is one thing to know, with your mind, what is right and what is wrong. It is quite another to live according to that standard. But, in living life that way, and acknowledging God's work in your life - that the good is not from you - then you will stand firm. You will not be disgraced; God will help you and the enemies will fade away.

I experienced another example of how we cannot, and do not need to, know the reasons. We just need to trust God. I attend the local Writers Festival each year and, as usual, I collected the program and selected the events I wanted to attend. I scheduled my availability to volunteer around these events, and awaited confirmation. Regardless, there was one event that had a fee that I wanted to attend and so I knew I should register before it filled up.

I tried, something between my Wi-Fi and Ticketek was down. Then I decided I would wait until next pay day. I just kept getting this feeling not to buy the ticket yet. So, common sense kicked in and I tried to explain it. Am I required to be a volunteer at that time? Is it part of the free offer to volunteers? Is something going to prevent me? Am I not meant to listen to this speaker? Should I attend another event in that same timeslot? I could not come up with any logical explanation as to why I shouldn't book my ticket. So, finally, I was able to.

Less than a week later, the festival was cancelled due to the Coronavirus outbreak. God knew I wouldn't be going to the festival. I could not possibly have foreseen a global pandemic or the way our government would react to it. God tried to tell me. I tried to use logic.

Water for the Minister

I sat in church one Sunday listening intently to the Minister preach his sermon. Suddenly, I noticed he had a bit of a dry throat and God said to me, "Go and get him some water". Being human, my first reaction was logic - "God, someone puts water under the pulpit every week, who am I to assume they made a mistake". Again, he simply said, "Go and get him some water". So, I obeyed the voice within and went to the kitchen and poured a glass of water, then humbly (eyes to the ground) took it up the aisle, up the stairs and handed it to the minister.

I was not to know that the person who puts the water there every week was away that day. The Minister was refreshed, and God got the glory. Notice, I didn't bound up the stairs with my chest puffed out, this wasn't about me at all. It was between God and the minister, I was simply the shell, the tool God used that day. Don't ever forget, that if he wanted to, God could simply make a glass of water appear there, but if he did that ten years ago, I wouldn't have had the example of knowing God that I can share today.

The result:
- The minister knew that God was looking after him;
- The new people in the congregation saw an act of kindness and love;
- I learnt about God's will;
- I got closer to God by having a visual, tactile miracle evidencing that I heard his voice.

The second time this happened to me was the same but in a different church and, once again it was about God, not me. This time, I humbly obeyed and just got the water, no questions asked.

The third time this kind of thing happened was not for the minister, it was a lesson for me, to teach me the difference between God's type of help and man's type of help. And, thankfully, I learnt it before any embarrassment!

I sat in church, listening to the sermon, when the minister started to cough, I took that as the 'oh-so-familiar' sign he needed water, right? God had trained me for this situation, so I knew what to do. Before I could move, he looked under the pulpit for water but didn't reach in for any. "Ah," I thought "I'd better go and get him some water, he obviously doesn't have any and he needs some." Then, seconds later, the minister reached under the pulpit and pulled out the glass of water. I sat there confused.

Yes, the minister realised that he would soon need a drink, and was checking to see where the water was, but he didn't want to break his thought train or interrupt the congregation's listening, so he kept talking and waited for the end of that passage.

If I had gotten him the water, these are the consequences:
- I would have interrupted the minister and the congregation's thoughts;
- The congregation would have noticed me, not a miracle of God;
- I would have missed the important part of the message;
- I would have been highly embarrassed, no not important but still valuable.

Can you see how this last example was unlike the first? In the first one, God got the glory not man, and a genuine service of help was given. In the first one, God told me to do it. In the third, I thought it was a good idea.

Key Points:
- Don't be quick to assume all experiences are the same;
- See things through the eyes of others;
- Be willing to accept that you are not always correct;
- Thank God for not granting your desires - he knows best;
- Avoid embarrassment, be sure it's God's idea and not yours.

Application for Chapter 6: Preparing yourself for the Job

1. Re-read the job description in this chapter.
   What do you mostly:
   Dislike _____
   Like   _____

   What parts make you:
   Excited   _____
   Bored   _____

2. Apply for the job advertised in this chapter. On another sheet of paper, select a section of the ad and write a half page application, explaining why you should get this job.

3. Congratulations! You got the job! Your new title is God's Helper. What are the first 5 things you want to do in your new role?

   _____
   _____
   _____

4. What combination of experience and skills makes you 'unique' in your family, workplace, or neighbourhood?

   _____

5. Select one Bible reference mentioned in this chapter. Write it out on another piece of paper and put it on your fridge. Memorise it this week. How can this verse change the way you can adjust your time, work, and priorities?

   _____

   _____

6. Look at the table for preparing yourself for the job. How can you prepare yourself for your new role,

Mentally	_____
Practically	_____
Spiritually	_____

7. Ask God now to help you start each day with the prayer, "Lord, what do *you* want me to do today?" Feel free to make any notes here that resulted from that prayer time.

   _____

   _____

Part 3: Salvation through the GIFT…

Hopefully, you are convinced by now that the great God almighty has chosen *you* to be the vessel for him to work wonderful things through. But now that your spiritual ego has expanded, I want you to change your attitude to your role. Remember the Belief-Expectation Cycle, "changing your attitude changes your behaviour". Yes, he wants to work through you, but that doesn't mean that you simply get to sit back and wait for Him to do it. He has already *done it*. He gave you a gift. The onus is now on you to open that gift, acknowledge that gift, appreciate that gift, and decide what to do with that gift.

Will you treat this it like an ugly tie and hide it in the back of the drawer until you can properly dispose of it? Will you treat it like a love letter, handwritten specifically for you, taking it to your chest and reading every word over and over with tears of joy, privately in your room? Will you treat it like a uniquely crafted diamond ring and wear it with pride, showing everyone that crosses your path?

I want you to look on this gift as an honour to possess. God wrote his Christmas list and purchased this gift for *you*. He hand-wrapped it for *you*. Once you realise this, you will see that, like a lot of Christmas presents, the gift that God has given you comes with responsibility, training and resources. After you have fully acknowledged what you have received, I challenge you to desire the best gift. Not the biggest, boldest, most expensive shiny gift. The *best* gift for you.

Salvation through the GIFT...

Chapter 7: Don't Underestimate the Power of Prayer

Do you access the power of prayer when doing his work? In the workplace, we tend to utilise the resources that the employer provides. Only a few companies require you to bring in essential items from home. I worked in a place where we had to provide our own pens and tissues. In another, office staff had to bring their own coffee. Relating this to God in a positive way, we bring parts of ourselves to the workplace, but he provides what we really need.

Pray to be used

In 2 Chronicles 1: 10 Solomon asked God to, "Give me wisdom and knowledge, that I may lead this people, for who is able to govern this great people of yours?"

How do you think God would reply to a request like that? Verse 11 tells us. "God said to Solomon, 'Since this is your heart's desire and you have not asked for wealth, riches or honour, nor for the death of your enemies, and since you have not asked for a long life but for wisdom and knowledge to govern my people over whom I have made you king, therefore wisdom and knowledge will be given you."

God answers prayers that are in line with his plans, not our selfish whims. The answering of Solomon's prayer was not just for his benefit. In 2 Chronicles 9:23 we see that, "All the kings of the earth sought audience with Solomon to hear the wisdom God had put in his heart."

Knowing the power of prayer, and the love of God, later Solomon instructs his people how to pray. The order in which

God responds to prayers is seen in 2 Chronicles 7:14-15 where, "If my people, who are called by my name, will *humble* themselves and *pray* and *seek* my face and *turn* from their wicked ways...". These are the pre-requisites to prayers being answered because it continues ... "*Then* will I hear from heaven and will *forgive their sin* and will heal their land. Now my eyes will be open and my ears *attentive to the prayers* offered in this place."

So, what is the order of prayer? Firstly, we are to be humble ourselves, pray, seek him intimately, and turn from our sins. Secondly, *then* God will hear us, forgive our sins, and heal our land – tend to the big issues first. Finally, *then* God will tend to our prayers.

In 2 Chronicles 13:13-18 we read, "They cried out to the Lord. The priests blew their trumpets and the men of Judah raised the battle cry. At the sound of the battle cry, God routed Jeroboam and ... God delivered them into their hands ... Judah was victorious because they relied on the Lord, the God of their fathers."

Often, when we are reading or listening, we hear the parts we like to hear. From this passage we take the message: cry out... God saves. And while that is ultimately true, there are many other steps in between. God can, but doesn't usually, just 'do magic' and make everything better. He wants us to call out to him, to trust him within the process. This helps others to see the victory, it allows us to have the victory, to give him the glory for it, and to go through some change as a result. All this from prayer! Even if the result of a situation seems to be the same whether we pray or not, there is much to be gained from going through it with God.

I have a recording in my journal from 16th May 2018 about a parcel delivery. It says this:

Ron was expecting a parcel today and someone had to be home to receive it. On my way home from my morning coffee walk, I remembered that this person was me. I then remembered that couriers deliver early in our area, so I started praying. I know sometimes God likes us to be specific, so I prayed that I'd be home *and* get the parcel.

As I turned into our street, I saw the delivery man go into the house over the road - a nice delay. Thanks God. As I reached my driveway, he was coming out and so he was walking towards me. This perfect timing meant that he saw me and so he called to me. He had already been to my house and had left a collection card, but ... now I have the parcel.

Thank you, God for perfect timing. This required - the neighbour ordering a parcel that was to be delivered by that company on that exact day; me doing the short walk, not the long one I had been doing; the delivery driver and I being within view of each other - only 2 seconds before or after and he wouldn't have seen me. And I get to tell him, "Thank God for perfect timing".

I don't think it is a coincidence that my journal entry from that night starts, "That was a good day!" and lists the good things that happened. And the next morning's entry starts with "I am feeling *so* excited!"

What do these stories have in common? They involve aspects of life that provide opportunities to include God in your journey. God has already given you all the resources you need. We know that he wants you to desire the best gifts. God wants us to ask for the tools to do the work he has asked us to do. Don't become complacent in a role, relationship or task. Instead, seek God's help always, to do the job to the best of his ability, not your own. The more time you spend with him, the better you will know his plans and know what to pray for.

In the words of Helen Keller, "I long to accomplish a great and noble task, but it is my chief duty to accomplish small tasks as if they were great and noble ... the world is moved along, not only by the mighty shoves of the heroes, but also by the aggregate of the tiny pushes of each honest worker." It is not feasible that we all be leaders. It is not possible for us to be the best at everything. God meets us where we are at and remember that he loves to use the underdog. (I think he enjoys the challenge.)

So, pray for the needy to be helped and healed; pray for their salvation and for them to have a closer relationship with God; pray for protection against the enemy. "Arise, Lord! Lift up your hand, O God. Do not forget the helpless." (Psalm 10:12).

Remember, this is God's work for the people and land that he created. This is not for me, I'm just a shell for him to work through. I have a responsibility to pray for those who need help, be it practical, spiritual, physical, or emotional help.

As you care for others, take their needs to God until they are able to do that themselves. "In my distress I called to the Lord; I cried to my God for help." (Psalm 18:6).

We are told in Romans 8:26 that, "The Spirit helps us in our weakness. We do not know what we ought to pray, but the Spirit himself intercedes for us with groans that words cannot express."

God would like to use us - humans, helpers - as he uses the Holy Spirit to assist others in their weakness. The Spirit can aid our hearts to prayer as we aid others' minds, thoughts and lives to salvation. Wow.

When praying please remember:
- Don't start the conversation asking for help, but for forgiveness. Don't make your prayer life just about you and your needs. Make it about your relationship with God, with the aim of getting to know him better. This is how you can

best represent him and be a suitable channel for him to work through.

- He already knows your every need. When we break down our needs to him, it helps us to clarify and prioritise. He wants us to be specific in our requests, but he does not need you to tell him what he already knows. How better could you discuss your problems with God?
- He promises to look after even the sparrows. Know who you are to him, you are a child of the living God, created and chosen by the great God Almighty. He longs for you to let him into your life so he can love you the best way.
- Humility brings us closer to him. Don't try and tell God how he should do things. Don't adamantly claim healing if God's best plan is that others get saved through their illness. Accept that you cannot know all the details, intentions, purposes or plans.
- Humility changes our priorities. Reminding yourself of your place in this world will keep your priorities aligned with his so you don't greedily ask for things like Ferraris, rather than asking for a way to help someone.
- Prayer is meant to be about communication, not self-gratification. Don't spend your time just asking for things you want. You wouldn't do it to a human, why do it to God.

Key Points:

- God wants us to ask for the tools to do his work;
- The more time you spend with him, the better you will know his plans, and know what to pray for;
- Pray to be used;
- Desire the best gifts;
- Access the power of prayer when doing his work.

The Difference

Imagine two people are in a room. They are both the same height, weight and strength. One is standing on a chair, the other on the floor in front. The one on the chair believes they can pull the other person up onto this platform with them, that things will then be okay for them. Sadly, no matter how much they pull, the one on the floor is going to pull the one on the chair down to their level, *not* the other way around. Don't stand on your moral 'high-horse' and preach at people, and be careful of the methods you use to assist others.

Insurance companies in Australia have a bad reputation. There is usually unforeseeable fine print that means they don't have to pay out. Renewing my insurance policy helped me see again that the difference between God and me is massive, and I need his help. In looking for car insurance only he knows if I'll need to lodge a claim and the details of it; the fine print and if the company will pay; all the hidden costs; and their company culture and internal policies affecting claims.

In short, only God knows the best policy for me and my *future* circumstances. So, I can choose to take advantage of his inside knowledge and ask for his help in making my decision. Or, I can ignore him and do it my way. I recommend doing it God's way.

God wants to help us, and he wants us to seek out his way of doing things. The Levites were entrusted with bringing the Ark of the Covenant to the tent but were quickly reminded about seeking his way. In 1 Chronicles 15:13-15 we learn, "It was because you, the Levites, did not bring it up the first time … we did not enquire of God how to do it …" But afterwards they carried the Ark, "in accordance with the word of the Lord". And the result was seen in 15:25b-26a, "with rejoicing … God had helped the Levites who were carrying the Ark of the covenant of the Lord … ".

Then in 2 Chronicles 15:12-15, "They entered into a covenant to seek the Lord ... with all their heart and soul ... They took an oath to the Lord with loud acclamation ... wholeheartedly ... they sought God eagerly and he was found by them. So, the Lord gave them rest on every side."

God has given us the gift of himself by giving us access to him.

The Difference, author unknown
> *I got up early one morning and rushed right into the day;*
> *I had so much to accomplish that I didn't have time to pray.*
> *Problems just tumbled about me and heavier came each task;*
> *"Why doesn't God help me?" I wondered. He said, "But you didn't ask."*
> *I wanted to see joy and beauty, but the day toiled on grey and bleak;*
> *I wondered "Why didn't God show me?" He said, "but you didn't seek."*
> *I tried to come into God's presence, I used all my keys in the lock.*
> *God gently and lovingly chided "My child, you didn't knock."*
> *I woke up early this morning and paused before entering the day.*
> *I had so much to accomplish that I had to take time to pray.*

This poem shows us how different a life can be when it is shared with God. The extreme opposite of that, the essence of evil, is twisting what God has given us. We see it today in many of the core elements he created such as marriage, work and food. Even love and helping get twisted and, generally, the motivation is self-centredness and greed. Many people live their lives with the expectation that, "it's all about *me* and what I want *now*."

Today we are taught to love who? Ourselves! So, as love gets twisted and the motive changes from God to us, from helping others to what can we get out of this, we see the human motivation to help others change dramatically too.

The way people think has changed through time. They don't ask themselves, what is the right thing to do here, or, what is the godly thing to do here. Instead they ask, what will I get out of it or, why should I help them. Even those who act generously often start their assistance around the thinking: what do I think this person needs.

Picture an addict, someone who is struggling to quit cocaine or cigarettes or alcohol. As their addiction is calling out to them and their moods swing, they ask you for "just one". Their world is crumbling, and you're confronted by their pain. Do you give it to them? It is what they want. It is their choice.

No, giving in is not the best way to help them in the long term. And we need to look long term. Their life will be so much better once they have beaten the control this thing has over them. You see, the gifts that we give to people are not always good for them.

Also, you are only offering them temporary pleasure or relief by submitting to it. We know the results won't last and they will then be looking for another fix. The world needs to stop looking at the now and start looking towards the long-term goals, both here on earth and eternity in heaven.

Don't think that you alone are making this decision. The Father of Lies, the greatest deceiver, is influencing both you and the unfortunate addict. And he would much rather you "help" in a way that hinders or enables the recipient to get worse. Then he has the victory.

So, the solution to this example is to allow the Father of Heaven to influence you in your decision making. What would God have you do here? What would Jesus do in this situation? What help will genuinely *help* this person on their road to recovery and to heaven?

God taught me about gifts and the ways the Father of Lies twists God's plans in an unexpected conversation. I had heard a horrific story on the news, and I asked God how people could be so bad. He told me, "For the *gifts* of the enemy are lust, anger, mental anguish, greed, violence, debauchery, idolatry, murder and self-loathing". I thought his word choice of was strange. He called these disgusting things that Satan provides 'gifts', and he started with the word 'for'. It was in writing them, that I saw the association with the Biblical language associated with his gifts. Each are the direct opposite of the gifts of the spirit. In all things, Satan will imitate, twist and deceive - lie.

Gifts of the Spirit	*Gifts of the enemy*
Love	Lust
Joy	Anger
Peace	Mental Anguish
Patience	Greed
Kindness	Violence
Goodness	Debauchery
Faithfulness	Idolatry
Gentleness	Murder
Self-Control	Self-loathing

Satan certainly is the father of lies!

Key Points:
- Only God knows the hidden agenda behind the fine print;
- Only God knows the best plan for your future circumstances;
- Know that you are not alone in decision making;
- The very essence of evil is twisting what God has given us;
- Ensure your decisions are influenced by the Father of Heaven not the Father of Lies;

Nothing else is reliable anyway

We depend on other people, computers, weather, money and parents, but we really can't rely on anything but God. Nothing else is truly reliable - people get side-tracked, they forget, and their priorities don't align with our own.

We are told in 2 Chronicles 16:12 that Asa had a severe disease but he, "Did not seek help from the Lord, but only from the physicians"; he suffered for two years then died. We need to accept that some won't want help, others won't want God.

How then, can we know when to help, when not to, or when to stop? It is our responsibility to be in God's will, and to have our prayers align with his desires and plans. If we falter from that, we will wander around aimlessly with the burden of not fulfilling his plan and not helping his chosen people. Who wants to face that in heaven! Put simply, we need to get our lives into his will! And then we will get the answers we need to clean up our lives so that we can hear God.

Have you ever gotten home from a shopping trip and realised that you needed something that you didn't buy only to remember, "I thought of that in the store"? That was your loving father trying to prompt you into submission. Too often, I have heard his reminder and tried to apply my own knowledge or logic. I try to picture the pantry shelf or fridge and then I decide whether

I really need it. At other times I simply don't give that little voice enough credence to follow through with the prompting. Then I get home and regret it.

If we can hear that little voice and obey in the little things, not only will our lives run a lot smoother, but we will become open to hearing his voice on the big matters that ultimately affect other people's eternal destiny.

One gentleman was told to cross the road. He did but nothing happened. This continued for several days until one day, he spoke to another person on the other side. This person died shortly after. God was testing his servant in little tasks - like obedience in crossing the road - so he knew he was ready for the bigger tasks that contain more responsibility.

Now, I'm not saying to run around and clear out all the ungodly stuff in your house, stop all your bad habits and end all the friendships with non-Christians. God can use anything he chooses to in order to bring good. The result may be that you do those same things, but do them under God's instructions, not yours. Seek God, come closer to God, get to know him better and wait on his directions for you, your lifestyle and your relationships. Are you married to a non-Christian? Don't file for divorce because he or she is not in God's will. Do you know God well enough to know what his will is? You may be the best opportunity God has to reach that person and lead them to salvation, but you may also be a hindrance to that cause. The point is, apply God's desires, not yours. The goal should be to seek God, don't seek what you think God's plan is.

I have heard debates as to whether God should answer the prayers of the Christians. One side says that God, "hears the prayers of the righteous" (Proverbs 15:29) and we are his righteous, so he should answer. The other says that we are here to serve God and he is not our waiter; we should not expect him to serve us. In no way does God have to help us. He wants to. remember, Jesus chose to serve and wash the feet of other people.

How about a compromise? If we are living in his will, we will know him through prayer, teaching and the Word. If we know him and his desires, then our prayers won't be selfish prayers (such as 'I want a Mercedes') they will be prayers such as, "please help me provide for that person's hungry children", "Lord, do you want me to teach Sunday School?", "Father, who should I witness to today and how?". The prayers of the righteous are prayers that Jesus would pray. After all, he is our example. So, if your prayers aren't answered, maybe you don't know God as well as you thought you did. And, how can you be doing his will if you don't know his will and don't ask Him what his will is.

I urge you to get to know God better.

Get to know God the Father, as both 'God' and 'Father'. The daddy that we all need to cry to sometimes, the father that is the head of the house, that has the ultimate responsibility over us and has our best interests at heart, the daddy that wants only the best for us and will do everything he possibly can to see that we have that. God, the creator of this universe we live in, the one who has the power to move mountains when he wants to, the one who designed and gave us the very sun that provides the light with which we could simply not live without. The one who has access to the past, the present and the future and intertwines lives and experiences to assist us with whatever plan he has for us.

Get to know Jesus, who suffered as we could never imagine for two reasons. Firstly, to show the world that he has the power to enable us to come close to him - eternally and here on earth - to tear down the need to go through ministers to reach God, so that we could know him and the Father personally. Secondly, so that no-one ever could claim that Jesus didn't know what they went through. Jesus is a caring, empathetic listener, who has suffered in every way physically, emotionally and spiritually that any person could ever suffer. He doubted, he cried, he grieved, he stressed, he gave. He never sinned.

Get to know the Holy Spirit. It surprises me that today when people want quick access, an easy life, and someone else to do things for them, why don't people want access to the Holy Spirit. He has immediate access to all the wisdom, power and love of both the Father and Jesus. He is with us constantly, and answers questions and requests so quickly no committee to go through, no submissions to write. He is just there, willing and able to help us on this journey called life.

Acts 16: 9-15 Paul had a vision to "come over to Macedonia to help us." He met a woman there and converted her. Be obedient to God's call. The result is that others will have the opportunity to be saved - because nothing else is reliable anyway.

Key Points:

- It is my responsibility to be in his will so my prayers will reflect his desires;
- Seek God, get to know him better and operate under his instructions for your lifestyle, actions and relationships;
- God will test us in little, so we are ready for the big;
- God has access to the past, present and future and wants to assist us with whatever plan he has for us;
- The Holy Spirit has access to all wisdom, power and love and is constantly with us, willing and able to help us through life.

Don't leave it to the 'experts'

"Be shepherds of God's flock that is under your care, serving as overseers - not because you must, but because you are willing, as God wants you to be; not greedy for money, but eager to serve." (1 Peter 5:2).

There are plenty of organisations that make a comfortable living from, and are happy to charge for, helping people - counsellors, financial planners, babysitters, mechanics to name a few. The world revolves around commerce (finance and business). That is not God's way. If we go back to the very beginning, God gave Eve to Adam, he gave them the Garden of Eden, and he gave them all the food and resources they would need.

Did Jesus have a large bank account with enough money to buy food to feed the 5,000? Did he pay to get out of jail or to hire a good lawyer? Did he pay doctors or surgeons to care for the sick? No, he trusted his Father to do his will to help those people he cared about. That is the commission that he has given us: to trust the Father to do his will to help those people he cares about.

We are instructed in Matthew 6:19-21, "Do not store up for yourselves treasures on earth, where moth and rust destroy, and where thieves break in and steal. But store up for yourselves treasures in heaven where moth and rust do not destroy, and where thieves do not break in and steal. For where your treasure is, there your heart will be also."

George Mueller was a man with a heart to do God's work. He opened five orphanages and housed 2,000 children at once, all without a cent to pay for it. Whilst doing God's work he prayed, and God provided the means to do the job. That's the key: we need to know that what we are doing is God's plan, not ours!

This story is not just a great story about helping children in need, it is a very powerful prayer story. You see, George and his wife prayed for everything on their list, and God provided it all: beds, linen, clothes, saucepans and food. Everything was donated to the orphanage and the doors were ready to open.

Their focus was providing a home for the homeless children in the area and so they hadn't specifically prayed for the arrival of the children. On opening day, they stood at the doors and waited, ready to welcome them all. No children arrived. Not one. Then they realised that they hadn't asked God to bring the children, and they prayed. They opened the doors on the second day, and the orphanage was then full.

In 2 Kings 5 we read about Naaman, a commander of the army and a great man. We read of his suffering with leprosy, and the various attempts to cure it. The king of Aram believed that the prophet in Samaria would cure him, so sent his commander to him with a letter of request. The king of Israel at that time had no faith, responding with rage and distrust.

Elisha heard about the situation and stepped in, telling Naaman to go and wash seven times in the Jordan River. But Naaman, probably feeling unwell and frustrated by now, expected God's healing method to be more direct. Verse 11 says, "I thought that he would surely come out to me and stand and call on the name of the Lord his God, wave his hand over the spot and cure me of my leprosy." He went off angry, sulking about one river not being any better than another.

But in verse 13, his servant pointed out a very simple truth to Naaman. "If the prophet had told you to do some great thing, would you not have done it?"

Isn't that true, that we tend to see the little things as insignificant and not worthy of "our" time?

We read about the *healing* in the very next verse. "So he went down and dipped himself in the Jordan seven times. As the man of God had told him, and his flesh was restored and became clean like that of a young boy."

We see the *result* in the next verse. "Now I know there is no God in all the world except in Israel." That's not how we would word it today, but his testimony was declaring that he had witnessed a miracle from God.

Naaman had a need and he sought God's help, God selected the tools – Elisha and the Jordan River – then he cured the leprosy and Naaman praised God. He later went on to tell Elisha that he would never again make any offerings or sacrifices to any god but the Lord.

You see, the result of Naaman's illness wasn't healing. It was salvation. His healing was a tool that enabled witnessing to himself, others, and readers of the Bible since then. Salvation is the last step in the cycle. And all of this was achieved by using the *correct* river, rather than a university degree.

Hairdressers have a reputation for being chatty and I usually try to engage in their stories. I was hunting for a new salon and was able to get in to see a lovely young lady.

Somehow, we went from talking about how happy and settled she was in her new town, to the struggle that she had been through to get here. I was grateful for her openness about her partner and his struggle with bipolar.

It struck me how supportive and patient she was with a man who clearly had anger issues, so I went deeper. "What in your life led you to not only live with, but embrace, a man who others would clearly leave?" She told me about her life growing up. Her grandfather had bipolar and her brother is autistic.

Many would say that she had been dealt a hard life, that she couldn't get a break from the stress. Others would argue that she would be right in leaving her partner so she can look after her own rights and safety first. Some would focus on just how hard her life has been.

But she took the difficulties of her childhood and used them in her adulthood. She took the knowledge and skills she had personally learnt, and turned them into tools to use when living with another person with the same, and similar, debilitating disease. This whole experience had made her a loving, patient, skilled, appreciative, accepting, giving human being. A helper.

Would those families have been better off if God had protected them from these experiences? I think not. I think God chose a great tool here in my new hairdresser, a tool that thinks selflessly and blesses others.

Did she need a qualification to become this person? No. I am grateful she became a qualified hairdresser, so I had the pleasure of meeting her. Did she need to consult textbooks, psychologists and doctors? She probably has chosen to do all of that to deepen her understanding. But none of but those tools made her the person she is. God did. She has a willingness to use her experiences to help others.

This is God at work.

Key Points:
- Trust God to do his will to help those he cares about;
- We need to know that what we are doing is God's plan, not ours;
- Don't think the insignificant is not worthy of 'your' time;
- Healing isn't the last step, salvation is;
- We are not better off being protected from bad experiences.

Application for Chapter 7: Don't underestimate the power of prayer

1. List 5 areas where you depend on other people. Are they 100% guaranteed reliable at all times? Are you relying on God to work through them or are you relying on them and their abilities alone?

   _____

   _____

2. What resources do you have at home that you could take to the workplace with you, and what resources does God provide for you?

   I provide: _____

   God provides: _____

3. Can you identify different types of needs in people? Briefly note people who have different struggles. If this is going to be seen by others, then don't write names, just an identifier like initials, a nickname or an alias.

   Need Type / Person / Specific need

   Practical   A:_____

   Spiritual   B:_____

   Physical   C:_____

   Emotional   D:_____

   Financial   E:_____

4. God has already given you all the resources you need. He wants you to *desire* the best gifts. What more could you be doing with the talents you have?

   _____

   _____

5. Select one Bible reference mentioned in this chapter. Write it out on another piece of paper and put it on your fridge. Memorise it this week. Now, write it here in your own words.

   _____

   _____

6. Identify one area of life around you that has been twisted – a relationship, a workplace situation, someone's need for medication or their greed or selfishness. Write down in 10 words or less what the problem is. Pray fervently for God's intervention in the evil that has taken what was his and twisted it.

   _____

   _____

7. Pray without asking for anything for yourself. Spend time talking with God, with the aim of getting to know him better.

Salvation through the GIFT...

Chapter 8: All the Resources

Welcome. You are the latest gift in God's kingdom.

For my 51st birthday, I invited everyone who was special to me and I gave multiple gifts to each of them. For those who couldn't attend, I pre-booked appointments to see them in the days after and delivered their gifts to their workplaces. I wanted to show them that I appreciate and love each of them. Many would say that my birthday should have been about me, but I wouldn't be me without them. They each played a part in me being who I am. They are all unique resources that helped me reach the age of 51.

God gave you many gifts - salvation of Jesus, the Holy Spirit, spiritual gifts, talents and air to breathe. These are not just for your use and enjoyment. He wants you to use these as resources to give to others, to help them to salvation.

You are God's Office

Imagine you are setting up a new business. You have the ideas, access to the resources and you know who your customers are going to be. The first thing you need is an office to operate out of. To gather your resources, you need your office to have the room to receive and store the supplies. To reach your customers, you need the office to have certain facilities - communications such as phone and email, an opening door - and advertising is always good. At times you may need extra staff.

We are reminded in Ephesians 2:10 that we are not doing this alone: "For we are God's handiwork, created in Christ Jesus to do good works, which God prepared in advance for us to do."

You are God's office! He knows what he wants in the shop, he has all the resources required to do the job, and he knows what every customer wants and needs.

As his office, he wants to put his resources in us - patience, Bible knowledge, skills, love, money ... any and every tool to do his job. He just needs us to allow him to use our communication facilities - our feet to go where he wants us to go, our mouth to speak when he wants us to, our hands to hold and hug as he directs.

We are told in 2 Corinthians 9:8 that, "God is able to bless you abundantly, so that in all things at all times, having all that you need, you will abound in every good work."

We are also his advertising, his billboard sign. He knows every customer and needs us to be available to take the memo and deliver the message or goods to those he is supplying them to. Just as we wouldn't go to a secular workplace and use the resources for our own benefit, God's gifts are not for our purpose but for his glory and the benefit of others.

Like the secular workplace, but to a much greater extent, we benefit personally from the experience of performing the tasks the boss has set us to do. We learn new skills in each job that we can then transfer to other tasks and workplaces. At the end of our career, we should be very mature, learned, skilled, experienced and employable in our profession - as God's Helper.

You are not only a tool working in God's office. You are God's workplace. His office. In Daniel chapter 2, we read about Daniel interpreting the king's dream. But, as Daniel explained to the king in verse 30, "This mystery has been revealed to me, not because I have greater wisdom than other living men, but so that you, O king, may know the interpretation and that you may understand what went through your mind."

Daniel knew that God's gifts are not for our own edification, but so that others can be helped and come to know God.

"Now that you have purified yourselves by obeying the truth so that you have sincere love for your brothers, love one another deeply, from the heart." (1 Peter 1:22).

Humans tend to get caught up in conditional love. Love is fundamental to God's message, the key to his entire being. The love he wants to show others is his love, therefore we must be able to receive, hold, show and teach sincere love, deep love, from-the-heart love.

The adage is true, "you cannot love others, if you do not first love yourself". To be able to receive God's love you must first accept that God made you. As I repeatedly told my children when they were growing up, "God made you and God doesn't make mistakes".

People come in all forms - tall, short, brown, white, blonde, brunette, outgoing, introvert, academic, sporty - the list is endless. The list of variables within the human race is infinite and, not once has God made a mistake in its creation. We have varied the original product and we have definitely made mistakes in doing that, but God never made a mistake.

So, if God is perfect and God doesn't make mistakes, and you accept that God made you, how can you not love yourself? Too many people struggle with this. Yes, we can hate the sin that is within us, in fact he tells us to. The closer we get to God, the more we become like him. The more we see our faults and confess our sins, the more we do his will instead of our own. The closer to perfect we become, *and* our focus becomes God-centred instead of Me-centred. *Then* we learn to love ourselves. "We love because he first loved us" (I John 4:19).

Now, move out from there. If God didn't make a mistake making you and you should therefore love yourself, it stands to reason that you should love others. If you are willing to see others as God sees them, then you cannot *not* love them. Look at them as God-created beings, hate the sin in them, but empathise with them for suffering under that sin and pray for them to be rid of it.

Don't even try to love them in your *own strength*, humans just cannot love everyone. Only God can *truly* love other people. Therefore, by treating other people as customers in God's shop, you should treat them with the patience and respect that he would if he were serving them directly instead of through you.

In his "Alive to God" daily message, Pastor Andrew Roebert explained it well when he wrote about Ephesians 3:16, "I pray that from His glorious, unlimited resources He will empower you with *inner strength* through His Spirit."

On 6th April 2018 he expanded on this verse, saying:

- "Did you realise that the Lord is the source of glorious, unlimited resources?
- Out of all his unlimited resources, he wants to come and strengthen you;
- He knows exactly what you need in your situation;
- By his Spirit, he wants to come and empower you from within."

There are times when God needs something done and we humans get in the way, so he simply must intervene.

Most mornings I go for a walk, one of two routes, the second a bit longer than the first option. As I approached the decision-making turnoff a couple of weeks ago, I was debating, making excuses as to why I was entitled to take the shorter option when God told me, "No shortcuts".

So, I walked past the turnoff and took the longer way home. It's funny, I was the one who decided that my body needed exercise, and I was the one who decided that the longer walk would be better for me. Are you noticing all the self in this process? Yet, I still try to talk myself out of it, justifying why I should - or should not - take the longer route that is better for me. So, if we *both* want me to go the longer way, why do I question, doubt, baulk...? Because I am human, and weak, and selfish and ... need I go on? Thank you, God, for your intervention, when I am not only letting you down, but me as well.

Sometimes *we struggle* with decision making. We see both sides and we argue with ourselves. If only it was always as easy as it was in 1 Samuel 3:15-17. God woke Samuel to give him a vision concerning Eli. As it was bad news, Samuel was, understandably, hesitant about sharing it with Eli. God took the decision making out of his hands by having Eli ask him directly, "What did he say? Do not hide it from me." God knows what we struggle with and will take the responsibility from us when it is too much.

Key Points:

- You are God's office, containing all the resources for his work;
- We are God's communication facilities;
- God made you and God doesn't make mistakes;
- Treat people as if they were God's customers;
- Sometimes we struggle with decision making.

Faithfully administering God

It is made clear in 1 Peter 4:10 that, "Each one should use whatever gift he has received to serve others, faithfully administering God's grace in its various forms."

My sister was asked to run the Sunday Minimites activities. Minimites are the children in church aged 2-5 and this job involved planning and implementing a program that included a story, craft, games and other activities. She agreed initially because she was willing to help but then the reality started to set in, and the panic levels started to rise. Weeks passed, and she stressed over what to do, how to do it and, eventually, how to get out of it.

Teaching toddlers was not her gift. She has raised her own children beautifully, and she had babysat for friends and my children on many occasions, so the problem was not the children or her interaction with them. The problem was that a human had given a role to another human that God did not want that person to do.

It is imperative that we ask God who he has in mind for what role before we ask them. If we don't, then we are trusting ourselves and other people instead of God, and we end up burdening people with the wrong duties. My sister would have done the job if necessary, but God did not call us to stress, he called us to do things his way!

Now let's look at the last part of that verse, "faithfully administering". An administration role is different to the role of an Administrator, but the common thread is that they organise, facilitate and manage the behind-the-scene formalities of an operation. Take, for example, a service office such as a Real Estate or Solicitor's. There will probably be a receptionist at the counter and at least one person out the back doing the paperwork of the senior personnel.

The senior personnel have duties and responsibilities that the administration staff member/s have only a glimpse of, and the administration staff have an understanding of the forms and compliance that the Senior Personnel may not have. They all need each other, and there should be a mutual respect for one another, because each perform their roles for the betterment of the company.

Coming from their role and perspective, the administration staff may have ideas about improving or changing things.

Sometimes the senior staff will implement these, but sometimes they just know, from knowledge and experience, things that the administration staff simply don't know or don't have access to. Although the senior staff get paid a lot more because they carry a lot more responsibility and have a different skillset, the administration staff are a crucial part of the company.

How important would the duties of the administration staff be if they were working for the Prime Minister? They are doing the same type of tasks, but each task touches more people and their boss carries more responsibility, and they spend more time in the limelight.

So, can you imagine being one of the administration staff for God? Think about it. Consider the duties involved. There are no forms, but there certainly is compliance, customer relations, time management and record management. What do we do with the data that is the Bible?

This book is not the right forum to discuss the Gift of Administration, but in this verse, we are told to *faithfully administer God*. Though we don't manage his whereabouts, we should know where he is at, and what he is doing, at all times. If he is working on a project, we should be ready and able to be an active part of it. When others need to talk to him, we need to know how to arrange that meeting and have The Book ready to consult. We should know his clients, not as intimately as he does, but certainly to a level that they trust us to mediate and pass messages back and forth whenever the need arises (prayer). We are to represent the company always, even when not on duty. I am sure I am not the only employee who has stopped what she was working on to drive a folder to their boss three hours away.

Some workplaces have magnets and uniforms with the company name and logo on them. These are tools to advertise the company. Do you wear a uniform? They are more common. Would your boss provide you with a company magnet or paint job for your private car? These can be more expensive, and more permanent. These are used in your private life, away from your employer. Does your boss trust you enough, to represent their company, their reputation, when you are not officially on duty?

Can God trust you to represent his company? Now, in your job as God's Helper, how are you administrating the tasks he has set you to do?

Samuel took a stone (pillar) as a symbol and said, "Thus far has the Lord helped me." (1 Samuel 7:12). We could all benefit from setting up *visual reminders* of God's help, and symbols that express our love and appreciation. Maybe you could do with a few more posters, plaques, or clothing items that publicly acknowledge God in your life.

Samuel didn't consider this to be the end of his journey, or the end of God's help. He acknowledged that God had helped him to this point, "thus far". While keeping focus on the big picture, we need to break each project into sections. Look at each portion, each journey, each phase of your life and acknowledge God's help in, and purpose for, each section. Then put it in perspective and accept how big, and how small, this particular component is.

As a new mum, I was still learning *the rules* when my firstborn wanted to sleep with me when I thought he was too old for this. My initial thought was, "This would be embarrassing if other mums found out my two-year-old still sleeps with his mummy". Then I realised, he won't want to sleep with me when he's 21. This is just a phase. Besides, if he needed that comfort, then I was the one to provide it.

Life is full of phases. Like the first time he lied, it didn't make him a liar. My child was not going to be a pathological liar, he simply told an untruth. I rested in the words that *'this too shall pass'*. And it did.

I learned then that we need to be willing to change with the phases of life. Backups in the 1980s were done on floppy disks that fit into the A drive on a computer. Then we had CDs, then EHDs, then USBs, and now the cloud. There is no point in backing up your valuable data onto a floppy disk anymore because you won't be able to access it.

While we may not like or understand the constant changes in technology, the point is that things in life do change and it helps no one if we stay stagnant. If we are not moving forward, we are moving backward. To administer God faithfully, we need to stay aware of the changes around us.

In James 2:14-17 we are challenged, "What good is it my brothers, if a man claims to have faith but has no deeds? Can such faith save him? Suppose a brother or sister is without clothes and daily food. If one of you says to him, 'Go, I wish you well; keep warm and well fed,' but does nothing about his physical needs, what good is it? In the same way, faith by itself, if it is not accompanied by action, is dead."

In other words, if you are not willing to give to other people to help them, then don't even bother praying. If you are not willing to do a task the boss has given you, then maybe you should leave that job. If you are not willing to love and help others with the gifts God has given you then you need to re-evaluate your position in his service. Sometimes we all need a real check up from the neck up.

Key Points:

- It's imperative that we discuss roles with God before we accept or delegate them;
- God doesn't call us to stress, he calls us to do things his way;
- We are to represent God's business here on earth;
- We need to stay aware of change - in people and in processes;
- If you're not willing to give to help someone, then don't even bother praying for their help.

Meeting them where God meets them ... where they're at!

Do you still marvel at how God meets your needs in the precise way that you need help right at that exact time? Are you often surprised when you think you're not ready for something, but God makes it happen? These things happen because he meets you at your level. He doesn't need to wait for you to be perfect.

That is exactly what we need to do for others. We need to meet people where they are. So, you need to forget all your preconceptions, training, assumptions and ideas and ask God "Where is this person? What do they need? What can I do?"

Remember, *only* God knows what they are going through, the experiences that led them to this point, how they are coping with their current situation and exactly what, where and how they need help. So why would we try to guess - when the one who knows is waiting for us to approach him.

What good is praying for a carpark at Coles and then driving to Woolworths in the next suburb? What good is speaking gentle kind words in French to someone who only understands English?

Never assume that people can't change their role. Do you

remember the café owner who needed help after her husband died? Two years later, she was the one literally sustaining lives. She nearly lost her house during the 2020 January wildfires, but that wasn't the worst of what she endured. Not once, but twice, the wildfires tore through her café property. She didn't run, she didn't quit. Her response was to feed - for free - all the firefighters working in the rural area of Putty. She kept her café open and cooked, with fires at three sides, to sustain the men and women who were protecting properties. This is the epitome of help. She didn't do it for the recognition or the money. She did it purely because there was a need, and she was in a position to help. In Deuteronomy 24:19-22 Moses instructs us of the simple attitude we are to have when helping other people. Helping is using the gifts God gave us to help people the way he wants to help them. It is done without any reward. It is done without embarrassing or guilting the recipient. It is to be done humbly and remembering that we once had nothing.

"When you are harvesting in your field and you overlook a sheaf, do not go back to get it. Leave it for the alien [person foreign to this land, not from outer space], the fatherless and the widow, so that the Lord your God may bless you in all the work of your hands. When you beat the olives from your trees, do not go over the branches a second time. Leave what remains for the alien, the fatherless and the widow. When you harvest the grapes in your vineyard, do not go over the vines again. Leave what remains for the alien, the fatherless and the widow. Remember that you were slaves in Egypt. That is why I command you to do this."

This attitude is quite different today. Everywhere we look, in every business transaction and private interaction, we see personal greed. Years ago, my mum told me a news story about a plastic bottle manufacturer. They apparently removed 1mm from each of the lids to save millions of dollars in plastic each year, hence increasing their profits. It made the bottles leak and almost impossible to open, but the company made more money. They weren't concerned about the customer, just the bottom line.

God can give and take, enrich or starve, bless or curse.

I hope by now you understand that whatever tools you possess are not by your own making or for your own good. I hope you realise that God gives you, and can take away, all the talents, tools and opportunities as he chooses. So, we need to value these gifts rather than take them for granted.

God has always considered these skills and tools to be of great importance. Even way back in the beginning of time, he had the scribes record, not only people's heritage and tribe, but the skills and tools that they had. One such example is seen in Genesis 4:20-22 where we are told of a family who, "… live in tents and raise livestock … play harp and flute…forged all kinds of tools out of bronze and iron…"

These skills were all useful, were used for the benefit of all, were not purely for self-gain and greed - lessons we could learn today. And not everyone had every skill.

There are 60 types of skills or jobs mentioned in Genesis and Exodus alone. Let's look at the range of skills in this list. Some are obviously considered to be "of better standing" than others. Some are professions, while others are talents. Some are foundational, while others are more luxurious. Interestingly, in some form or other, they nearly all still exist today.

Animal handler / ruler	Perfumer
Baker	Personal adviser
Brickmaking	Pharaoh
Builder	Pharaoh's army
Captain of the guard	Pharaohs officials
Carpenter	Physicians
Chief baker	Priests
Chief servant	Prince
Chiefs	Prison warden
Commander of the forces	Prostitute
Commissioners	Seamstress
Concubines	Second in charge
Cupbearer	Servant Shearers
Dignitaries	Shepherd
Elders	Skilled craftsmen
Herdsmen / Horsemen	Slave drivers
Hunter	Slave girl / woman
Judges	Slave masters
King	Sorcerers / Sorceress
Leaders	Spies
Magician	Steward
Maidservant/Manservant	Tent maker
Maker of spices and balms	Tool maker
Maritime people	Tribal rulers
Midwife	Warrior
Musician	Wine maker
Officials	Wise men

Of course, in the New Testament, we see that the tools God gives us are more often referred to as spiritual gifts, but these are still for the same purpose - to be a resource to help others get into heaven!

Key Points:
- Only God knows exactly where someone is at and what they need;
- Do not embarrass or guilt; rather, help humbly, remembering you once had nothing;
- Helping is using the gifts God gave us to help people the way he wants to help them;
- Whatever tools you possess are not by your own making or for your own good;
- God gave, and he can take away, all the talents, tools and opportunities.

Money is a tool, not a motive

After driving away from visiting my brother and his girlfriend, I went to the local cinema and bought them two movie tickets. They weren't expecting this, and I didn't embarrass them by knocking on their door. I simply returned and put the envelope in their mailbox.

Later, he messaged me saying he didn't know how to say thank you. I don't know if they went to the movies, but I did learn something from the experience. One of the main reasons why my family had given up on my brother was because he was "a user" - he was always asking for money. But he would never have asked for the money for a movie ticket. And, when I bought those tickets, the cost didn't matter. The money didn't matter. I bought those tickets because I wanted to give love. The money was simply the tool necessary to provide that.

God's gifts are not for our edification, but so that others can be helped and come to know God. We see in Daniel 2:30 and 47 that, "This mystery has been revealed to me, not because I have greater wisdom than other living men, but so that you, O king, may know the interpretation and that you may understand what went through your mind."

"The king said to Daniel, "Surely your God is the God of gods and the Lord of kings and a revealer of mysteries, for you were able to reveal this mystery."

God's goal is *always* salvation and he will use whatever resources are required, be it money or mystery. Even in 1 Corinthians chapter 5 when he says to remove the sinner from the church, it was so he will be saved. Verse 5 says to, "Hand this man over to Satan, so that the sinful nature may be destroyed, and his spirit saved on the day of the Lord."

Luke 6:32-36 speaks of loving your enemies and explains how even sinners loan to whom they expect repayment, and love those who love them. Jesus asks us to loan our possessions to others without expecting repayment. In verse 35, he specifically tells us to, "Love your enemies, do good to them, and lend to them without expecting to get anything back." This is the attitude we should have.

I know a couple who give by not taking.

The husband is self-employed, and his wife does the bookwork. Together they decided that, if any work is done for less than the original quote, they deduct the difference from the final invoice. They refuse to take money unnecessarily.

I cannot think of any other business that would do that, certainly none that I have ever been involved with. Even if a business realises they are making more profit than expected, they would not acknowledge that to the customer. Their response *may* be "Oh, let me give you a discount." But their motive is so you will think they are generous and praise them to others and ultimately buy more from them. Not once in that transaction do they think about the customer!

Furthermore, Solomon tells us in Proverbs 14:31 that, "He who oppresses the poor shows contempt for their Maker, but whoever is kind to the needy honors God." It shouldn't be a hard decision, should it.

I have a history of organising businesses. It's just what I do. So, it's not an ego thing when I offer to help a business or community group get their systems in place. I often do this voluntarily, with the result being that they earn money, not me. I enjoy it. I love to use my experience and skills to *help* a business and its personnel.

In 2 Chronicles 31, we read about tithing and the distribution of it. Verse 8 is a great example of how to bless man and glorify God. "When Hezekiah and his officials came and saw the heaps, they praised the Lord and blessed his people Israel."

Then in verse 20, "This is what Hezekiah did throughout Judah, doing what was good and right and faithful before the Lord his God. In everything that he undertook in the service of God's temple and in obedience to the law and the commands, he sought his God and worked wholeheartedly. And so he prospered."

The tithe given was grains and wines, oil and honey, herds and flocks. Hezekiah could have selfishly made himself rich but instead, he even contributed from his own possessions and then distributed it among the people.

Sometimes, people require practical knowledge and experience. Other times, their needs are emotional support. Neither form of giving costs the giver - a little time, money that would have been spent anyway, a cheery conversation and maybe a hug. None of this is an inconvenience to the giver but can be life changing for the recipient. What's more, none of them are from a textbook or are well structured. They result from simply having your heart and mind open to using what God has already given you, at a time when he brings a need to your attention.

Key Points:
- Money is merely one tool to enable us to give love;
- God's goal is always salvation, and he will use whatever resources that requires;
- You can give by not taking;
- Giving of your finances is the same as giving of your time or other assets;
- Giving is not done 'by the book', it is having your heart and mind open for God to share what he has loaned to you.

Application for Chapter 8: All the Resources

1. List 10 resources that God has given to you.

   _____

   _____

   _____

   _____

2. Look at the list of skills and jobs from the Bible. Thinking of your skills and passions, what three jobs would you like?

   _____

   _____

3. In what ways can you give to others by not taking?

   _____

   _____

4. Let's be creative. Imagine God says this to you: "_____, I have been training you for this next phase of your life. I need you to open a bricks and mortar business in your town using what I have taught you so far."

   What type of business would it be?

   _____

What would your role be? _____

What are the top three goals? _____

_____

5. Select one Bible reference mentioned in this chapter. Write it out on another piece of paper and put it on your fridge. Memorise it this week. What does this verse mean to you personally?

_____

_____

6. How can you keep practising what you have learned this week?

_____

_____

7. Have a 'Staff Meeting' with God. For his business to reach its goals (love, helping, salvation…) what is on the agenda for you to implement? Feel free to make any notes here that resulted from that prayer time.

_____

_____

Salvation through the GIFT…

Chapter 9: Desire the Best Gift

Excited? Good, but don't sit back and rest on your laurels. Don't become complacent. Like painting a room or learning a new subject, once you start, you realise how much more there is to do. There is never enough time to do it all. Take a moment now and hand over to God all your interests, desires and passions.

Eagerly desire the best gifts

Salvation through the *gift* of help … it's an unusual phrase, isn't it? We know salvation is God's plan. We know he wants to work through us to help people. We know he gifts us with every possible resource to do that. But combined, it still sounds strange.

Why do you give presents at Christmas, birthdays or weddings? Generally, because you love and care for the recipients, who are usually special people who you have a close relationship with. God wants his children to enjoy such a relationship with him and so he wants to treat us with gifts as well.

It's easier to buy a gift for a sibling than for a sibling's new partner you hardly know. That's because we like to make gifts appropriate and personal, something that will be enjoyed and appreciated by the receiver.

Do you recall me saying that God allows us to experience things so that we have empathy and skills to help others going through the same type of experience? In a way, these experiences are gifts to us so that we can regift the benefits to others. Just as you carefully select the gifts you give to those you know and love, so too does God.

He chooses what gifts, experiences and opportunities to give to each person. And he chooses to give this gift to you. His gift to you may have been the strength that became your ability to withstand a car accident or a rape. That gift, now in your possession, can be used to help others. Don't waste it or hide it. Ask God how you can use it for its intended purpose.

Let's not try to use those gifts without the instructions though.

In 1 Corinthians 12:31 we are told to, "Eagerly desire the greater gifts". What good is owning every imaginable musical instrument if you have no desire to play? God gives us access to his precious gifts but wants us to desire them. In fact, God doesn't just *want us* to desire them, he has *called us* all to *desire* the gifts.

What's more, God places these gifted people within certain churches, communities and towns so that the collective can work for his purpose. We all fit together to make the body of Christ and, like any group, each member has different responsibilities. No wonder the body of Christ hasn't fulfilled its function here on earth. The body is falling apart. It doesn't work together. Some parts are stronger and overpower the others. Some parts lag behind. What an image you get if you take this literally - one foot going one way, a hand racing off in front ... We need to desire the greatest gifts so that we can fulfil God's plan in our part of the world.

Paul told the Corinthians in Acts 20:35, "In *everything* I did, I *showed* you that by *this kind* of *hard work* we must *help the weak*, remembering the words the Lord Jesus himself said: *'It is more blessed to give than to receive'*." Let's break this verse down and consider how we can apply it today.

Everything - In every part of every aspect of my life, in all of my actions;

I showed you - I lead by example, teaching others;

This kind - I must be an example;

Hard work - It isn't easy doing God's work, but then, the life Jesus chose for 33 years wasn't easy either;

Help the weak - Not just those with an illness or injury, but those who don't have the strength and capabilities for their situation (mentally, financially, spiritually or intellectually);

Remembering Jesus - Our motivation to help people is much bigger than just solving their current crisis, and so the gifts we give should be more than just immediate and material;

Giving - Most of God's gifts to us are intangible, yet we tend to like gifts that we can wrap up. Start thinking of gifts to give to meet people's needs that cannot be wrapped.

Often, we look only at the obvious. We look at the problem not the cause. Men are often criticised for this, for going into 'fix it' mode rather than listening to what their spouse 'really' needs. We are very good at putting Band-Aids on sores.

Think of a young child who daily comes in with grazes from falling off his bike. Of course, you tend to the wounds, but it may be necessary to also spend some time training him, adjusting the seat or tyre pressure, or changing the area he is riding.

When we ask for help, God knows that the answer isn't always in simply solving that situation. God doesn't just answer what we ask for. He goes above and beyond that because he knows what truly needs repairing for total and permanent healing.

We need to keep this in mind when we are helping other people. Look deeper, pray harder, before giving your help to someone in need. Others can help them pack to move to a new house. You be the one who buys them their first groceries. Others can take them a meal or drive them to the doctor when they are sick. You be the one to help their child with homework because they are too weary.

I am not instructing you to do these things, I am not arrogant enough to say that these are the better methods. I am not saying don't provide the initial responses as well. What I am saying is, when you become aware of a need, seek God's input. Then you will respond to their need in a way that draws their attention to the loving God who wants to help them. Helping others is not about you getting the accolades. What glory does God get if you do what every other person is capable of. God needs to stand out while you go unnoticed!

In Psalm 68:5-6a God is, "A father to the fatherless, a defender of widows…God sets the lonely in families…" He doesn't merely provide them with a meal, he gives them the ultimate gift for their need. This is our goal.

Dare to be different, desire the best gifts for the person God has led you to help.

Do you hear his voice calling?

To be able to hear God when he gives you instructions, you must be tuned in to his voice. Visit a hospital and listen to the babies, can you identify them? No. Now, give birth to a baby and listen to the dozen babies cry in the maternity ward. Can you tell which one is yours? Not immediately, but you learn to. Five years later, enter a playground or stand outside the classroom door and listen to the kids play and you can hear your child's laugh over all the others. Why? Because you have spent so much time with your child that you recognise their voice even when you can't see them. This is how it is with our relationship with God. We need to spend time with him, getting to know him and his voice so we can hear it amongst the other sounds around us.

Key Points:

- Don't hide your gifts, ask God how to use them for their intended purpose;
- Give gifts that cannot be wrapped;
- God needs to stand out while you go unnoticed;
- Desire the best gifts so you can provide the ultimate gift of help to others for their need;
- Spend time with God so you recognise his voice above all other noise.

Pay it forward

Often at special occasions such as Christmas, we find ourselves in the situation of *keeping up with the Jones'*. We buy gifts for people only because we know they will be buying for us. Or, we spend more than we should because we know they will be giving us an expensive gift and we feel we need to match it.

God doesn't want you to do a good deed for someone else purely because someone did a good deed for you. I hope by now you have realised that God wants you to be available; that he offers you every resource to do the job; and he wants you to be willing to accept the gifts he offers. It's time to put this in motion.

Have you seen the movie *Pay It Forward?* Basically, it is about receiving a blessing where, rather than returning a blessing to the giver, you pay it forward by blessing someone else. In doing so, you pay forward the attitude of thanksgiving and give to someone who God has placed in your path. Someone you know nothing about.

After this movie gained popularity, I heard a story about a customer in a McDonalds drive-through restaurant who paid for the lunch of the person in the car behind. The second driver was so surprised and blessed that they paid for the order of the car behind them. This continued for 17 cars! Now think about that. Each customer probably spent no more than they had planned to anyway, so no-one was out of pocket. Yet, 17 people received *double blessings* - the blessing of receiving and the blessing of giving. You know that warm feeling of satisfaction when you give a surprise, do you agree that it far outweighs the feeling from receiving?

Being a helper, giving to others, helping others, being used by God, being close to the Holy Spirit, and working in the miracles of God are all to *bless people and glorify God*. They are not for our satisfaction, glory, ego or benefit at all. As you come to know God, you realise that things of this world are not that important. They are temporary and often distract us from the real purpose of life. Being a Christian, you are assured of your eternal salvation. So, the purpose of helping and using God's gifts is not for the purpose of getting you to heaven. The purpose is to help other people come to know God in a real way so they can experience the same salvation.

We are told not to hide our gifts. We know we shouldn't brag about them. We also need to be mindful not to use them selfishly. Don't try to use the gifts for your own gain, it won't work. Don't even bother trying, God knows the heart of man. You can fool others, you may even fool yourself, but you cannot fool him. Instead, we are to *protect and nurture* the gifts he has given us. Nurture the wisdom gained from an experience, a talent, or a person in your life.

There is a good reason why people are not allowed to enter competitions provided by the company for which they work. The competition is a tool used to draw new customers in and make people aware of the company. It introduces more people to the business and its services by showing them the friendly generosity of what the company is providing, in this case heaven. If the employees were the only ones to enter, they would have a good time and appreciate the prizes, but this would only further enhance the intricate bless-me club and no new people would come to know the Giver. The resources would only be circulated internally.

Liken this to heaven … we need to pay forward the gifts that are provided by God's 'company'. Don't keep them inhouse. Share what you've got, with the end goal to introduce others to the wonders on offer.

So, having access to God's resources is not for you. You have access so you can use them for others. In fact, 2 Corinthians 9:2 tells us to have, "Eagerness to help … ready to give … and your enthusiasm has stirred most of them to action." That's what God wants - our willingness to help, our eagerness, our enthusiasm. That's when he sees results.

If he simply handed out gifts to everyone easily, how many would truly appreciate them? How long would they last? God wants his people to appreciate the gifts he gives, not because he is conceited, but because he knows that these gifts are the keys to eternal life for the population and, as I said before, if you're longing to get to heaven quickly, you need to spread the message.

So, where does the role of helper fit into God's plan for salvation? How can baking a cake or teaching a skill help someone get to know God?

Psalm 30:10-12 tells us, "Hear, O Lord, and be merciful to me; O Lord, be my help. You turned my wailing into dancing; you removed my sackcloth and clothed me with joy, that my heart may sing to you and not be silent. O Lord my God, I will give you thanks forever."

Here again we see the cycle. Someone calls out to God for help, God hears and answers the need, changing the person forever, and the person praises God.

Note the use of the word 'that', the purpose of God helping is so *that my heart may sing to you and not be silent.* We are all to speak up and share the good news when God does good things for us. There is enough negativity in this world and, unfortunately, it tends to dominate most conversations. Why not claim the victory and share good news instead? Who knows, someone might just get saved as a result!

In Psalm 22:1, the King James Version tells us, "My God, my God, why hast thou forsaken me? Why art thou so far from *helping* me, and from the words of my roaring?" Whereas the NIV shows, "My God, my God, why have you forsaken me? Why are you so far from *saving* me, so far from the words of my groaning?"

Here we see another example where our literary and linguistic experts believe that these words are synonymous, that helping, almost literally, means saving.

Key Points:
- Giving is much better than receiving;
- God doesn't bless us just for our benefit;
- Assurance of salvation is the purpose of helping;
- Protect and nurture his gifts;
- Share good news in a negative world.

Don't try to master one gift

God is omnipotent and omnipresent and so you are most useful to him if you too can be anywhere at any time available to do anything. Don't restrict yourself to one type of service. Your skills may be required today to babysit, but don't allow yourself to be labelled as the local babysitter and then get so involved in Kids' Church and weekday crèche that you limit yourself from doing other services. Tomorrow he may want you to cook a meal for someone or go on the hospitality roster. Again, don't then run off on a tangent and spend all your time and focus solely on preparing meals for all your neighbours and fellow church goers, and then the local Soup Kitchen.

Whatever you are involved with, do it diligently, but be open and flexible, listening for God's next instruction.

Recently, I realised that my life of organising had become part of my identity. I was known as an organiser. I called myself an organiser. I love organising, but I was becoming less productive as my passion was lending itself more to planning than actually doing the task at hand. I had to learn that organising is a tool, only one tool, one ability that God gave me. Organising is not a job title; it is a skill. Once I got that back in perspective, I was able to spend less time organising and more time doing (in the organised manner I am used t, of course).

By giving yourself only to one method of service, you close your eyes, heart and mind to other services. You then miss the opportunities he puts before you to serve in a multitude of ways.

Remember, *he* gives you the skills so all he asks from you is your willingness to do what he asks, and your ability to hear him when he calls. On that note, let me remind you that time together is required for you to be tuned into his voice.

Psalm 121:1-2 says, "I lift up my eyes to the hills - where does my help come from? My help comes from the Lord, the Maker of heaven and earth." The best help that people receive doesn't come from a person, but from God himself. He prompts people to help, and gives them a heart to help.

God made the earth and people. He has the right to use them as he wants, irrespective of whether we see that purpose as good or bad. He uses trees for both shade and firewood; sun serves to grow and provide warm, as well as burn; and he uses man to help the planet and everything in it. The help is from God, through his shells, his helpers, us.

Just as he is flexible with the way he uses items from the earth, he is flexible in the jobs he has for us to do. In one project you may need to sow the seed, in another you may water them. To be at his service means being available for his service. It does not allow for us to put restrictions on his call. "Lord, I'm at your service when my neighbour needs help moving" is not enough. He has a much bigger plan, and many more opportunities than that. Don't limit your availability to the one who created it all.

Keep growing

It benefits everyone for a business to have staff that are both experienced and trained. Training is an ongoing tool. It includes staying abreast of changes in society, in customer problems and current solutions. It involves learning new skills, and new ways to solve customer problems. If you don't continue to train, you are at risk of being replaced by a more effective and efficient competitor. That competitor may not necessarily give better quality or service, but if they have something to entice the customer, than you may lose the customer.

Look at this in your role as helper. You need to ensure that your customers - the people God has brought to you - see something in you and your boss, God, so they come back. If you don't make your customers trust the service that you provide, they may be willing to look at other options, and these could include anything from cults, drug use or suicide. A little extreme yes, other examples include child abuse, violence and gambling.

For you to be able to understand what your customers need, you may need to have a look at the lives around you and do a little research into the temptations that people are succumbing to. What are the people in your area suffering with, what makes them hurt others or commit those crimes? Undertake some personal training into the lives of your local current and potential 'customers' - the people that God may ask you to serve.

Am I trying to scare you into thinking that you have other people's lives in your hands? No. You simply sit in God's hands with other people. You face them, get to know a little about them, catch them, hold them, offer them a tissue, hold their child … whatever is required at that time.

Remember that the gifts we possess are given of God, they are not our own. Acts 17:24-28 says, "The God who made the world and everything in it is the Lord of heaven and earth … gives all men life and breath and everything else … He is not far from each one of us. For in him we live and move and have our being." We cannot make ourselves good at anything. It is God who decides who will be able to do what. Yes, even those arrogant people or those highly educated people, God has allowed them to gain whatever skills he wants them to have. What they may not know yet is that God allows them to have skills for a reason. So that, one day, they may allow God to put them to use through their lives.

How to Grow as a Christian, **author unknown**

P*ray without ceasing (1 Thessalonians 5:17)*
R*ejoice in the Lord always (Phil 4:4)*
A*dd to your faith, virtue (2 Peter 1:5)*
Y*e have not because ye ask not (James 4:2)*

W*hatsoever He says to you, do it (John 2:5)*
O*nly fear the Lord and serve Him (1 Sam 12:24)*
R*emember the words of the Lord Jesus (Acts 20:35)*
K*eep yourself pure (1 Tim 5:22)*

G*o into all the world and preach (Mark 16:15)*
I*n all thy ways acknowledge Him (Prov 3:6)*
V*ow and pray to the Lord your God (Ps 76:11)*
E*ndure hardship as a good soldier of Christ (2 Tim 2:3)*

Look at the bigger picture

A young married couple decided to have a family close together and, as a result, gave birth to six beautiful children in the space of six years. Can you imagine the washing, cooking, and cleaning that had to be done? Now, these parents loved their children, there was no denying that. Dad was a good provider and mum stayed at home with the children. She played with them, talked with them and read them stories. Both parents participated a lot in the church life. Their only fault was they were … let's just say, they weren't house-proud. The washing covered most floors in the house, the washing-up sat there for days, beds were never made … are you getting the picture?

Now, because they were very involved in church life, they were highly valued by fellow Christians, and so it seemed fitting that the church ladies would help with the housework. After all, didn't God tell us to look after others? Isn't this book about helping others?

So, a few of the women decided to help the couple and clean their house. What a lovely gesture, don't you agree? At face value, yes. The problem was that the *ladies* decided, and God didn't. God has asked us all to keep clean (but be grateful we don't live in Old Testament times and have to keep all their laws!) so the result was fruitless. Within a week, the house was just as disgusting, and what's more, they never changed.

The messy house was a consequence of the parents' inappropriate priorities. It was these priorities that had to change, before any change could occur to the state of the kitchen or bathroom. I believe that, if God was in control, these parents would have learned from this refresh, and kept the house clean thereafter.

Maybe it would have been wiser for a church leader, such as a loving and tactful pastor's wife or another mature woman, to visit the home and teach the couple (especially the mum) housekeeping techniques, time management skills, or even to arrange a babysitter for a regular time so the couple could clean house together. In this case, teaching skills that will assist for the rest of their life would have been much more beneficial (and easier on future guests) than cleaning the house once!

There are many good books on prioritising God's work. If you are unsure, ask your local Christian bookstore.

Key Points:
- Don't limit your availability;
- Work diligently and flexibly, while listening for God's next instruction;
- In your role, you can stop people seeking alternatives;
- Lovely gestures aren't always helpful;
- Keep growing.

Don't quench the spirit

At a time when the black dog of depression was biting, my daily passage asked me to dream big about God's plan for the people in my life. My immediate response was basically, "There's nothing I can do. I can't fix people's lives. It's best if I stay out of it. But you, God, are powerful to do whatever you want to do."

You see, I believed in God, I just didn't believe in me. The next words I read were: "Rejoice always, pray continually, give thanks in all circumstances; for this is the Lord's will for you in Christ Jesus. Do not quench the spirit."

Then Romans 12:2 told me, "Do not conform any longer to the pattern of this world but be transformed by the renewing of your mind. Then you will be able to test and approve what God's will is - his good, pleasing and perfect will."

My job wasn't to fix other people's lives. My job wasn't to trust in my abilities, even if I do acknowledge my skills and abilities come from God. My job is to allow God to do what he wants to do through me. And to be able to hear and be directed, I need to know him better. To know him better, I need to spend time with him – I need to renew my mind.

God's plan for us is bigger than we can imagine. In the Old Testament are two characters, whose names I always confuse, but I am grateful for the lessons their existence teaches me.

Elisha's purpose and miracles happened because he didn't get what he wanted. In 2 Kings chapter 2, he followed Elijah until his death, then decided to head back to Gilgal. Elisha tried to replicate the miracle performed through Elijah by striking the water with the cloak and having it separate so he could cross. This worked for Elijah because it was in God's perfect timing. This time, however, God did not want Elisha to go home to Gilgal because he had miracles for him to do on *this* side of the water.

- The water was bad and unproductive. In response to the people's asking, God used Elisha to add salt, and the water was healed. Verse 21 tells us the result, "I have healed the water. Never again will it cause death or make the land unproductive.";
- Delinquent youths were destroyed on Mount Carmel;
- The widow was given a way to pay her debts and enough provisions to live on;
- The woman's child was brought back to life.

Then, after all these miracles and the faith that resulted in the spectators, Elisha returned to Gilgal. Of course, again, the timing was perfect. He was just in time for God to use him to heal the famine-stricken deadly food, so the people were not harmed. He used him as a tool to help a lot of people. Of course, Elisha hadn't sought God's direction, so God had to intervene, making it impossible for Elisha's plan to succeed. God will have his way and he had a much better purpose for Elisha.

Life is a bit like playing an electronic game. It seems to take a lot of time and effort to get a high score that is worth valuing.

Then, you continue to play but allow yourself to be distracted and, in an instant, one poor judgement, and bang. Game over. You're back to square one.

What if we valued our relationship with God, family, our morals, time and intelligence as a high score in a game. We would devote concentrated time to protect them. We need to constantly guard ourselves against distractions that can lead to us doing something wrong. These poor judgements can set us back immensely.

God made us exactly how he wanted us to be. He made us to be suitable to whatever purpose he had in mind and gave us the Holy Spirit to help with that. He also realised the value of humans helping one another, but it is us who interferes with his projects.

In the very beginning of the Bible we see God's plan for helping. He made the Garden of Eden and then made Adam, "To work it and take care of it". Adam's job was to look after it, to help it grow to its potential. Adam was to help the environment, the land and the animals.

Then, in Genesis 2:18 God decided, "It is not good for man to be alone. I will make a helper suitable for him." God had already made animals and birds, but they weren't suitable for the plan that God had for man.

Please allow me to digress here for a moment because, in my opinion, one of the funniest events in the Bible occurs here in the next few verses.

"Now the Lord God had formed out of the ground all the beasts of the field and all the birds of the air. He brought them to the man to see what he would name them; and whatever the man called each living creature, that was its name. So, the man gave names to all the livestock, the birds of the air and all the beasts of the field." Adam did what God wanted him to do, but his motive wasn't the same as God's. He wasn't just naming them, he was assessing them because of the preconceived expectation that the purpose of this was to find himself a suitable helper.

The very next verse is my favourite: "But for Adam no suitable helper was found." God promised Adam a suitable partner, but he didn't say he would supply it immediately. God thinks differently to us. After making his promise, the next thing God did in establishing his new world, was to continue his daily business and bring Adam the animals for naming.

But Adam, being human, assumed that everything was about him and that God would act instantly. So, he jumped to the conclusion that the next thing on God's list was to provide him with a partner. That's typical human thinking. Adam wasn't seeing this task the same way God was. He was disheartened because there wasn't a suitable helper among the animals! Of all the animals God put in front of him, like an assembly line, he found none that appealed to him to take on as a lifelong mate. I, for one, am very glad about that.

Adam didn't understand the concept of waiting and didn't consider that maybe God had other things to do as well. Of course, God knows everything in advance, and he certainly could have worked to Adam's agenda, but he had a better plan. I'm sure he has a sense of humour too.

"So, the Lord God caused the man to fall into a deep sleep; and while he was sleeping, he took one of the man's ribs" You know the rest; we then got Eve. I have this image in my mind of God laughing at Adam and deciding to 'knock him out' while God did the job he had already planned, the one Adam assumed incorrectly.

God didn't plan to give Adam a suitable helper from the animal kingdom. All along, he planned to give him a woman.

Adam couldn't imagine this because he hadn't seen a woman - he didn't know the full capabilities of God's work. He assumed, based on his limited human understanding, his own timeframe, and what was directly in front of him. God had something different in store for him. Something better. Something suitable.

Like Adam's helper, what makes us suitable is what makes us different. This passage shows us several ways we can desire the best gifts and not quench the spirit. It also shows us that our relationships with humans are meant to be distinct from those with animals. Unlike animals, we are not to be threatened or disposable (humans are not to be used for meat) nor should we have a killer instinct. He did not intend us to be animalistic and isolated. Instead, we are supposed to communicate using a higher level and we are to love intimately, not just to breed like animals.

We are to use our heart, mind and spirit - not just our body. Man leaves his parents and is united with his wife and the two are to "become one". Just as God provides individual helpers for specific purposes, we don't need to be the partner or helper to everyone. We help as God calls, in the places he puts us, as he assigns us the project. Try not to get in the way of the work God is doing.

Key Points:
- My job is to allow God to do his job through me;
- God's plan is bigger than our plan;
- We should value our relationship higher than any game score;
- Don't jump to assumptions with God;
- Our differences make us suitable for God's assignments.

Application for Chapter 9: Desire the Best Gift

1. List 3 ways you could 'pay it forward' this coming week?

   _____

   _____

2. Rank the gifts listed below in order of those you most desire

   ___ Communication   ___ Creativity

   ___ Empathy   ___ Help

   ___ Hospitality   ___ Teaching

   ___ Giving   ___ Love

3. Look at the world around you - your school, workplace or neighbourhood. Select one current situation, issue, or culture that you know little about. Now, what can you do to learn more about that? eg speak to a foreign neighbour, research a particular culture or addiction…

   _____

   _____

4. Write down 3 people you are going to give gifts to this year (birthday, Christmas, wedding…) and write an idea for a gift beside each one. There's a catch: each gift must benefit the recipient in some way, and none can be tangible / material.

   Person   **Gift**   **Benefit**
   _____
   _____
   _____

5. Select one Bible reference mentioned in this chapter. Write it out on another piece of paper and put it on your fridge. Memorise it this week. How can this verse change your way of seeing your relationship with God?

   _____
   _____
   _____

6. Is your attitude to helping other people changing at all? In what ways?

   _____
   _____

7. Talk to God about the gifts you desire and your ideas for using them. Wait on him for direction and then implement his ideas together.

220

Part 4: Salvation through the gift of HELP

The fourth and final step in the Belief-Expectation Cycle says: "Changing your behaviour changes your life". I hope you now believe that God wants to work through you to help others, leading to their salvation. To do this, you have collected the resources and accepted that the job is yours. It's time to look at your behaviour.

Helping: What is, and what is not, your responsibility? What is the right and wrong way to help? How much should you be available? Who should and shouldn't you help? How do you know when to say no? How do you protect yourself from being taken for granted or stretching yourself too thin? God doesn't give one answer to these questions because he is flexible, tending to humans and their situations individually.

So far, we have looked at salvation through the gift.

Part 1 showed us the cycle of help that leads to salvation, and that the ultimate example of helping is seen in God himself. It is his will that we should reflect his character and care for the people he created.

Then, in part 2, we looked at our role. Using the position description, we applied for the job of God's Helper, and learned that we are tools in God's toolkit for him to work through.

In part 3, with our job description explained, God reminded us who the boss is. Helping others is not something we do for ourselves, or by ourselves. We help others because God asks us to, because God has given us a heart for others, because God has given us the gifts and every resource required.

Now, in part 4, it's your turn to put the gifts God gave you to use, so that they can bless man and glorify God. This is not just about helping or doing; not in the way we are used to thinking about helping. This is doing it his way.

These last three chapters take us from being an overactive practical human helper, to living as the God-created, God-inspired, God-enabled helper that he made you to be. You are going to get on your knees, stop thinking like a human and get on with the job, trusting God is providing every resource along every step of the way. Trusting what we know, "That in all things God works for the good of those who love him" (Romans 8:28).

Salvation through the gift of HELP…

Chapter 10: Warning: Bad Help

The word 'help' is usually perceived as a good thing and, until now, I have been encouraging you to help people. So far, we have seen a few examples of getting it wrong, but now I challenge you to consider that helping can sometimes be a real hindrance. Yes, helping can be a bad thing. There are times when helping, though it may have brought immediate satisfaction, can do more harm than good.

Positive or Negative Help

What comes to your mind when you hear the word 'help'? We usually associate it with doing something nice for someone. For example,

- Helping an elderly neighbour with their groceries;
- Helping a friend to move to a new house;
- Helping a sick relative; or
- Helping a child learn to spell a new word.

What about the word 'positive'? It too, usually has nice connotations. People are often encouraged to "be happy, be positive". But being positive doesn't always mean being happy. I can be positive that grocery prices will rise, it doesn't mean I am happy about it. Sometimes, helping people won't make them feel happy. Your responsibility is to make sure your help is godly, useful and for the ultimate good, not just to appease a quick fix.

A good starting point is your thoughts: the words you choose to allow to dominate your mind. Before you think that sounds very harsh, I do understand that there are people who really struggle with negative self-talk, and I urge you to seek assistance for this. Do whatever is necessary so that God can be the victor over your mind. Start with the instruction of Philippians 4:8, "Whatever is true, whatever is noble, whatever is right, whatever is pure, whatever is lovely, whatever is admirable - if anything is excellent or praiseworthy - think about such things." Train your mind like you do your body, so that you have control over it, rather than it having control over you.

Addicts know that their substance use becomes a problem when it controls them rather than them controlling it. If it is possible for a person addicted to nicotine, alcohol or heroine to regain control over those powerful forces, then I ask you to seriously consider claiming control over your own mind.

Back when I had only two grandchildren, there was a period when a range of circumstances kept me from spending time with them.

Walking along one day, I watched a young boy interact with his mother and it brought sadness and longing for the youngsters I was unable to see. I started to feel like the victim, taken for granted, and tossed aside - blame, whinge, moan - and I knew too well the mental spiral this could take. It was time for me to make a decision.

Whether I felt sad or happy, those current conditions could not change. Irrespective of my mood, I was the one to suffer by thinking in a self-pitying way. Despite my circumstances, I had to try to prevent negative thoughts from gaining any momentum and control over me.

But the lesson learned was not just about the psychology of positive thinking. It was that it's okay to have a negative thought and feeling. It's what I do with them that matters. So, I took the sadness and the grieving and turned the emotion into a story. This helped me voice my feelings without hurting anyone else.

It gave me a productive way to spend my time and thoughts, and a sense of purpose by doing so. Many types of artists do this: musicians, painters, and writers.

Some negatives can be turned around. Some need to be utilised to help others who experience the same. All negative thoughts need to be addressed.

Negative thoughts - sad, depressing or judgemental - will pop into your head. Before you open your mouth and allow those words from your mind to become external words, check your motive, the context, and your relationship with God. Helpers carry the responsibility of speaking words that are encouraging, positive, uplifting and forgiving.

We often think it is our right and responsibility to chastise in order to teach people. That may be in some cases, but that discernment is a totally separate gift. Here, we are talking about helping, and tearing people down with brutal honesty helps very few. Yes, Jesus turned tables. Yes, God admonished and punished. They are God; you are human. So, before you tear someone apart, be very sure that you are in God's will and doing this in his will and in his strength. If in doubt, remember that God sees everything. How will you answer to him for the comment or instruction you are about to issue to another one of his children?

It is helpful to also seek God's instructions. He tells us how to think in Colossians 3:2, "Set your minds on things above, not on earthly things." God clearly wants our focus and priorities to be on godly attributes rather than worldly possessions. By doing this, we will naturally remove a lot of the negativity, the sadness, and the criticisms that attack ourselves and others.

A negative can be turned into a positive by changing your perspective. In the same way, a positive can easily landslide into a negative thought or state of mind. So, what is it that alters the outcome? Your point of view plays a big part. Try to turn negative thoughts around before they become actions; it is much better to act in a positive or productive manner, than to respond from a place of criticism or judgement.

When you are assessing the words in your head, be mindful that situations may not always be as they appear. Our interpretation may not always be trustworthy.

Also remember that. just because an event isn't successful or pleasant doesn't mean that God isn't in it. Look at the Old Testament. There are many examples where situations didn't appear to go well. We learn from our mistakes and we grow through trials. These are all part of God's plan. That's the key - to be a part of God's plan, not ours, in helping - whether it appears to suit our plans or not.

I have talked a lot about the Belief-Expectation Cycle and there is another similar verse I would like to share with you. I don't know who wrote this originally, so I cannot give credit for it. In fact, if you google the words, a lot of people have put their name to it. Regardless, it has certainly been a positive help to me throughout the years, so thank you to the author and to those who have spread this great message.

> *Watch your thoughts - they become words*
> *Watch your words - they become actions*
> *Watch your actions - they become habits*
> *Watch your habits - they become character*
> *Watch your character - it becomes your destiny.*

You see, our thoughts, words and actions can have both good and bad consequences. Our aim, of course, is to produce good.

The words of our God are powerful and permanent. Matthew 24:35 tells us that, "Heaven and earth will pass away, but my words will never pass away". Jesus himself said that everything else is temporary, except his words. The Bible has certainly been evidence of that. So, for stability and confidence, we should aim to know, focus on and share his words more than rely on our own.

In Exodus 23:1 God told Moses, "Do not spread false reports. Do not help a wicked man by being a malicious witness." This was one of the laws God gave for his people, so it is not to be taken lightly. From this example, we can see that carrying out the action of 'being a malicious witness', would be 'helping' a wicked man. Obviously, that would not help in a positive way and yet, the Lord uses the same word. Therefore help, be it positive or negative, means to assist, influence, cause others to do something.

In reality though, this is not always the case. The actions, or words, we do under the guise of helping someone can unfortunately do more harm than good. Bad help is doing the wrong thing, not necessarily a negative thing. Hence, it starts with thoughts. In Psalm 28:7 "My heart trusts in him, and I am helped." The helpee needs to trust God and the helper, it is as simple as that. The rest of this verse leads to joy and thanks to him in song.

Along with loving our children, the parents' role is to teach them how to be adults. How to be productive, loving, godly, descent people. Watching the news, I learned that apparently 60% of parents (interviewed) don't know that children should clean their teeth twice a day. Healthy babies are not born wanting sugar and yet, children as young as two are having teeth extracted because of the damage done from too much sugar. These parents probably love their children and want their children to feel happy (which is not the same as being happy) and so give into the cravings that they created in them.

We are told to, "Keep yourself pure" in 1 Timothy 5:22. Don't think you're helping someone by succumbing to their practices of witchcraft, smoking, swearing (or sugar). This is one of the biggest traps of this century, the belief that we need to lower our standards to avoid making others feel uncomfortable.

I studied with Lifeline Counselling years ago and debated this with one of the leaders. I didn't think that I had to swear even if my client did. Their teacher at the time said I should swear so my client feels comfortable and will open up to me. While it would be no good if I sat there like a stuck-up arrogant snob, I couldn't see that my swearing would convince them I was able to help them. Remember, people come to you for help because they believe you have something that's better than what they have, whether you have the answers, or a peace, or direction; they haven't gone to their peers for help, they've come to you.

The elders were told in 1 Timothy 5:21 to, "Keep these instructions without partiality, and to do nothing out of favouritism". Only God knows how each person will respond to help so trust him by following his instructions, be it the basics as recorded in the Bible, or specifics as he instructs you for a particular person or circumstance.

I urge you to strive towards a life where your words and actions result in positive effects or influences on others. God has given you the ability, and the awesome responsibility, to influence every person that you have contact with (directly and indirectly). Please make it positive - eternity is waiting for them, don't block their opportunity to share in that joyous comfort of salvation that you enjoy.

In Ephesians 4:29 we are told, "Do not let any unwholesome talk come out of your mouths, but only what is helpful for building others up according to their needs, that it may benefit those who listen."

Key Points:
- Being positive doesn't always mean being happy;
- All negative thoughts need to be addressed;
- Help - be it positive or negative - means to assist, influence, cause others to do something;
- Bad help is doing the wrong thing, not necessarily a negative thing;
- God has given you the ability, and responsibility, to influence every person you have contact with.

Help don't hinder

We adopted two magpies that we fed a couple of times each day. After a year, these two became parents and we were honoured to be introduced to their three babies. The parents took the easy road and had us provide food for all five of them, which we didn't mind because we loved interacting with nature and enjoyed their trust. But, once I realised that the babies weren't learning to forage for food themselves, I knew we had to withdraw. What had started out of love, could end up being dangerous. If they were totally dependent on us to provide their food, they would suffer and die when no-one was home. They needed to maintain their independence, and so we decided to ween back their rations.

Now, it would be cruel to suddenly stop feeding them, so we gradually decreased the amount and frequency, to force them to look elsewhere as well. These birds were never going to be permanent house pets, so they needed to maintain their survival instincts. The adults understood this and found food when we weren't at home, but the babies knew no different. Something had to change and had to be us, not them.

We were putting them at risk by feeding them. Kindness is not always kind. Helping is best done by doing what is best for the long term, not what appears nice at the time.

Best intentions

Often, well-meaning individuals say and do things that have an adverse effect on the recipient. Despite having the best intentions of supporting the other person, it is important that we don't assume to understand their personal predicament. While a person in a wheelchair may need assistance to get the item from the top shelf, don't automatically jump in to carry a bag for them. This may be one thing that makes them feel independent, possibly one technique they have spent a long time perfecting.

While being willing to help, don't assume either way - that a person who lives with chronic pain or other disability, can or cannot do something.

Jess suffers with chronic pain and a range of debilitating conditions, one of which is the difficulty to swallow tablets. She shared with me the most common scenario when migraines or back pain appear. Most people react by asking, "Have you taken your tablets?". Already in pain and suffering from aphasia (the inability to speak correctly), this is her thought process: "I would love to be able to take tablets to ease my pain, but right now, I cannot swallow them. This inability adds to my frustration, and also reminds me that I am not as able as you. Plus, now I feel like I have to justify myself to you." One simple question can create a myriad of self-doubt and anguish - and the person wanting to help had no idea.

I encourage you to ask God what this person needs and put aside what you think is the best course of action. Allow the Holy Spirit to guide you as to what this person needs you to do for them.

Doing It All for Them

In 2 Kings chapter 4 we read about the widow whose creditors were threatening to take her boys as slaves to recover her husband's debt. This woman was in need of help. We know God could have instantly wiped her debt, in one way or another, but he chose not to. Instead, this woman of faith witnessed a miracle, one similar to the New Testament story of the loaves and fishes.

This woman had a small amount of oil, but God made it continue to flow until there was enough. Verse 7 shows us, "Go, sell the oil and pay your debts. You and your sons can live on what is left."

God didn't make her a millionaire, and he didn't destroy the creditors or remove the debt. Instead, he worked a miracle that would be told for thousands of years. He taught her and her sons about faith and hard work, and provided enough to live, not indulge, but live comfortably.

It is good for people to work. It keeps us healthy, accountable and responsible. We get to contribute, be sociable, and feel productive and useful. In Luke 11:46 Jesus rebuked the lawyers saying, "And you experts in the law, woe to you, because you load people down with burdens they can hardly carry, and you yourselves will not lift one finger to help them."

When we do a task for another person, the intention is to help them, not to make it harder for them. Don't get caught up in legalism. Instead, use your own skills to help, not hinder, others.

Ruth helped Naomi. Boaz helped both by letting Ruth glean the harvest, and told his men not to touch her. He didn't just give her food; she had to work to gather it all. She was just protected under a watchful eye while doing it.

You've probably heard the saying, "Give a man a fish, you feed him for a day. Teach a man to fish, you feed him (and his family) for life". When God's in charge, something happens! And God's work brings long-lasting, eternal results, not just temporary satisfaction.

Doing as They Ask

One teenage girl lay on her bed having swallowed a box of her father's prescription drugs. Her sister-in-law entered the room, saw she was not in a good state and demanded, "What have you done?"

Several thoughts flashed into the mind of the teenager - getting in trouble, letting her parents down, her father needing these tablets, and not dying - and so her response was, "I've just taken 31, but don't tell anyone." Her sister-in-law had a choice: to tell or not to tell. She decided to do as she was asked, not tell anyone, so she didn't.

The girl was announced clinically dead upon arrival at the hospital. Her body was revived, and her stomach pumped. She was then in a coma for a week, before returning home. She was fortunate - she survived. A person needing help is not always in the best position to make the best decision.

We should consider the state of the mind of the person needing help. Chronic pain and depression are only two of the conditions that can cause a person not to think rationally. These sufferers often cannot ask you for the help they really need even if they can recognise what that is. If you know anyone suffering with health issues - mental or physical - please encourage them to have a written plan on their fridge or by their bed. A plan constructed when they are in good health negates some of the decision making later. Pain makes irrational, poor decisions.

Mia had watched a friend suffer with mental health throughout high school, and this young lady had taken to cutting herself. One day in year 11, Mia knew her friend was at risk and decided to stay with her instead of attending class. A head teacher approached and told them that school is the most important thing and they would be in trouble if they missed any. Under normal circumstances, in a school environment, this would be true. However, as her friend was not capable of putting forth any argument, Mia had to make a decision. She knew personally what this girl was struggling with, and what she would do if left alone or put under too much pressure. Mia chose to stay with her, preventing her from going to the bathroom and cutting herself, until she was stable enough to seek professional help later that day.

As a helper in situations like these, you are confronted with immediate crises and you cannot know all the details. At other times, you would call on someone with more experience such as a boss, an elder sibling, or a more experienced person. In times like these, it is imperative that we lean on God for direction, trusting that he, and he alone, knows the history, circumstances and purpose of the situation you and the victim currently find yourselves in.

Deliberate hindrances

Especially as the world worsens, there are those who will deliberately go out of their way to make people's lives harder.

Braydon rolled his ankle not once, but twice in two days. After school, his mother took him to the hospital and his foot was put into an ankle backslab. The next day was his first Naplan Test so he wanted to go to school. "It's a bit sore, but I'm okay," he told his mum.

During recess in the playground, a group of his peers noticed him hobbling and asked for details. These boys, armed with the knowledge of the injury and pain, made a decision to make his life worse. They thought it would be funny to jump on his injured foot. No logic. No good in it at all, other than their own pleasure of seeing another writhe in pain.

Braydon persevered through the rest of the day, and after school his mother took him back to the hospital. He now needed a full cast because the other boys had broken his foot.

I don't suspect any readers would do something like that, but you may be given the opportunity to discourage that type of behaviour. It also bears consideration: is there anything you do that may be hindering another?

Key Points:
- Eternity is waiting for them, don't block their opportunity;
- Helping is best done for long-term results, not immediate satisfaction;
- It is good to work, don't do it all for them;
- Pain leads to poor, irrational decisions;
- Consider what you may be doing that hinders other people.

Is it your responsibility?

Mary Kay Ash wrote, "There are three kinds of people in this world: those who make things happen, those who watch things happen, and those who wonder what happened."

Despite your initial reaction, the last kind may not necessarily be lazy. They may be uneducated in that particular aspect of life, or physically unable to help, or working so hard that they are too preoccupied to see what is happening. As humans, we can never know every detail of everything happening everywhere in the world. We must be careful not to be so quick to judge those who appear any less, in any way, than ourselves.

Assuming you want to be one of the first kind, the kind that makes things happen, there is one very important thing to know. Just because you see the need, does not mean that you are the one to fix it. By jumping in, you may actually be denying someone else the blessing that comes from helping. It's okay to delegate.

We are reminded in 1 Kings 8:18-19 that, just because we have an idea, doesn't mean it is our responsibility to fulfil it. David wanted to build a temple for God and, while God also wanted this built, it wasn't David, but his son, who would have the job.

"The Lord said ... you did well to have this in your heart. Nevertheless, you are not the one to build the temple."

Like David, it is important to identify your role. We read earlier that we need to 'watch your habits, they become your character.' What are your habits? What are you good at, known for, interested in? What's your persona, your role, your character?

Knowing your strengths is one part of a helper's role. Knowing when and how to help are just as important. Just because you are the one to identify the need, does not mean you are the one that has to answer the need directly. Maybe you are better off supervising, using your experience to know how or when the help is required, or delegating the task to a person that would be more accepted by the person in need. Perhaps a woman that has children is best to help another mother.

Again, the key is knowing God, doing it his way. God is the Project Manager. Let him assign the roles and responsibilities. In most cases, he already has. "Some teachers ..." He didn't say we should all teach.

1 Timothy 5:3-16 gives very practical straightforward advice on helping widows, both young and old. It's a long passage, but there is a lot to be learned from it.

> *Give proper recognition to those widows who are really in need. But if a widow has children or grandchildren, these should learn first of all to put their religion into practice by caring for their own family and so repaying their parents and grandparents, for this is pleasing to God. The widow who is really in need and left all alone puts her hope in God and continues night and day to pray and to ask God for help. But the widow who lives for pleasure is dead even while she lives. Give the people these instructions, too, so that no one may be open to blame. If anyone does not provide for his relatives, and especially for his immediate family, he has denied the faith and is worse than an unbeliever.*
>
> *No widow may be put on the list of widows unless she is over sixty, has been faithful to her husband, and is well known for her good deeds, such as bringing up children, showing hospitality, washing the feet of the saints, helping those in trouble and devoting herself to all kinds of good deeds.*
>
> *As for younger widows, do not put them on such a list. For when their sensual desires overcome their dedication to Christ, they want to marry. Thus, they bring judgment on themselves, because they have broken their first pledge. Besides, they get into the habit of being idle and going about from house to house. And not only do they become idlers, but also gossips and busybodies, saying things they ought not to. So, I counsel younger widows to marry, to have children, to manage their homes and to give the enemy no opportunity for slander. Some have in fact already turned away to follow Satan.*
>
> *If any woman who is a believer has widows in her family, she should help them and not let the church be burdened with them, so that the church can help those widows who are really in need.*

God loves every type of person mentioned in this passage, and urges us to show wisdom in who, and how, we help. The help should be provided from the right people. This passage clearly explains how help can be a hindrance.

God loves building character. It is good for everyone and has long-term benefits. Deuteronomy 22:4 tells us that, "If you see your brother's donkey or his ox fallen on the road, do not ignore it. Help him get it to its feet."

If we are confronted by a situation, we may tend to help because others are watching, but if there is no one around, how easy is it to pretend we didn't know about it, to ignore it. The world's attitude tends to be, "Hey, if there's no glory in it for me, why do it." Why? Simply because it is the right thing to do, it is good for us and the person requiring the help. Add to this, that God sees everything we do, including the intention of our heart, and he told us not to ignore it. So, why *not* do it?

I was confronted by this many years ago. I admit that I don't like housework. I'm not a slob, I like the house to be clean and tidy, but I would always rather be doing something else. There was a ball of paper under a chair and, although I noticed it, I walked on past. While not consciously, I had decided to leave it there. Part way out of the room, Jesus convicted me of this. "If you could see me present in this room, would you leave that there or pick it up?"

Now, if I was sharing a house with Jesus, of course I would pick it up. I would want everything to be as clean and tidy as possible. *Well ... aren't I?* I went back and picked up that paper and, from that day I have been convicted. Even if no-one else sees it, even if no-one else knows whether I see a mess, Jesus knows that I see it. He knows when I consider leaving it and so now, I always pick up any mess because *he is looking!* It is my responsibility.

Key Points:
- Just because you see the need, doesn't mean you're the one to fix it;
- It's okay to delegate;
- God is the Project Manager;
- God loves building character;
- Would you leave it if you saw Jesus sitting there?

Don't think you'll always get it right!

I have just told you that, just because you see a need, doesn't mean you are the one to fix it. I then told you not to leave a mess if you see it. Working with humans can be contradictory, which is exactly why I keep directing you to follow God's instructions, not your own. One fundamental principle is to do what is right in God's eyes, but don't think you will always get it right.

When I started on this book, I was living very close to God. As the years went on, like most Christians, my journey had its highs and lows. During those lows I wasn't game enough to work on the book because I didn't want *me* to ruin it. After all, it was his work and, if I wasn't spending a lot of quality time with him (as with any relationship) how could I know his intimate thoughts, ideas and plans for this project?

So, I hid it away like some people do with jewels and money. But who benefits if I have jewellery and cash hidden away in a safe deposit box or in a box under the bed? Nobody. Who benefits if I have a gift from God and I don't display it? Nobody. So, this book had to come back out and be completed.

However, who benefits if I use my money to bless other people by giving to them in their time of need? Lots of people.

Who benefits if I use my gift from God to bless others and lead them to a closer relationship with the God they will spend eternity with? Lots of people. In fact, as many people as we make time for.

I've said it before, but it's worth repeating: your talent is God's gift to you. What you do with it is your gift back to God.

Imagine God holding a list of names of people that have needs. How many of them do you think he wants to help? All of them, of course. How many of them do you think he can help? Again, all of them. Now, if he has chosen to use you as a tool to help those people, how many are you going to make yourself available for?

Consider: you're not saying 'no' to them. Oftentimes, they don't even know about you, your gift or the God who loves them. You are saying 'no' to God - just like Jonah did, and even he gave in eventually. God *will* have his way, how long and how hard the journey will be is entirely up to us.

So, I've since learnt to start each day, each writing session, with a prayer. "God, please help me to help you by writing this book to help people help other people." I acknowledge my dependence on him and my humble part in it. The point is, you won't always get it right, so don't be too harsh on yourself. Learn from your experiences and seek God's advice as to how to do it better next time.

It is very easy to offer the wrong type of help. When Miss X had a breakdown, her husband went to take care of the kids - packing their bags, picking the older ones up from school, and delivering them all to his sister's house for overnight care. What he didn't realise was that the mother needed the love and companionship of her children. She didn't need to be left alone to fend for herself while nurses stuck needles in her and doctors told her she'd never walk or talk again. She needed her husband and kids beside her.

Another young woman was suffering severely with depression. In fact, she was on the verge of having a breakdown, and she hit the alcohol seriously. Her friend tried to comfort her but, having lived a more sheltered life, she had no experience with depression or addiction. She wanted to help but she couldn't handle seeing her friend in that state. Feeling unable to do anything, she left.

Meanwhile, the patient deteriorated, and she knew from her past mental breakdowns that she needed the Mental Health Team. Sadly, in her state, asking for help confirmed her feelings of uselessness and her belief that she was a major inconvenience on others. She couldn't reach out for help. She was in no condition to be making decisions and, ideally, her friend should have stayed around until she found out how to help.

As I as mentioned before, I'd like to encourage all sufferers of physical and mental conditions to please leave instructions for family members, so they can make these decisions when you are incapable.

The absence of help can be helpful

"In the days of her affliction and wandering Jerusalem remembers all the treasures that were hers in days of old. When her people fell into enemy hands, there was no one to help her. Her enemies looked at her and laughed at her destruction." (Lamentations 1:7).

While I didn't have enemies laughing at me, (well, not that I know of) I did feel like I was wandering through the wilderness for many years. I felt alone and distant from the God I knew and longed to love again.

God is not there to answer our every whim. When living outside of his will, he can ensure that there is no-one to help, if that's the form of discipline necessary to teach and bring us closer to him. That's what helping is for, bringing people closer to him, and even the absence of help can be helpful. So, when things don't go according to your plans, instead of doubting or resenting, be grateful.

In Jeremiah 47:4 we read, "For the day has come to destroy all the Philistines and to cut off all survivors who could help Tyre and Sidon. The Lord is about to destroy the Philistines, the remnant from the coast of Caphtor."

There were people willing to help Tyre and Sidon, but God didn't want them to help such wicked people, so he intervened and made sure that their help didn't happen. God had a much bigger plan and knew a lot more than any of the decision-makers of the time. Please, let all help be from the Lord!

Not all help is accepted

God gave the promised land to the twelve tribes of Israel. Yet, upon arrival, two and a half tribes decided to stay on the east of the Jordan River rather than enter that promised land. They had wandered for 40 years to get there and now they were willing to fight for their right *not* to enter the land.

You can lead a horse to water, but you cannot make it drink. Some people simply won't take the help that's being offered. Don't be offended, sadly it's part of being a mere mortal. And don't judge, there could be valid reasons in their thinking, or it may be part of God's bigger plan. Maybe God is still dealing with issues like stubbornness.

I had asked God to help me get through three piles of paperwork. I got through two of them smoothly and then decided to go and watch a DVD, neglecting the third. Later that night, I realised what I had done and apologised for taking his help for granted. I had ignored the help he'd given me in response to me asking him for it! After I learnt my lesson, he then changed my schedule for the next day to accommodate my prayer. My point is that not everyone will respond as we expect them to.

Key Points:

- We cannot know his ideas and plans if we're not close to him;
- God will have his way, how long and hard the journey will be is up to us;
- The absence of help can be help;
- When emotionally involved, we can jump in and provide the wrong type of help;
- Some people simply will not accept the help.

Application for Chapter 10: Warning: Bad Help

1. Why does God not always respond in the way we expect?

   _____
   _____

2. Name some areas / ways we can 'do it all for them' eg pay their bills

   _____
   _____
   _____

3. Identify ways you have been 'helping' that are not useful, and you need to change

   _____
   _____
   _____

4. What could the recipients learn if you react differently?

   _____
   _____
   _____

5. Select one Bible reference mentioned in this chapter. Write it out on another piece of paper and put it on your fridge. Memorise it this week. Now, write it here in your own words.

_____

_____

_____

6. What part of your life do you react emotionally or immediately, rather than taking time to think and pray?

_____

_____

_____

7. Spend some time in prayer, discussing your method of helping people and ask for God's direction for future responses. Feel free to make any notes here that resulted from that prayer time.

_____

_____

_____

Salvation through the gift of HELP…

Chapter 11: The Needees' Needs

Forms of help cannot be boxed or presented into a nice neat list. There is no way I could prescribe ways to help in all the situations that you face. Nor do I have any intention of limiting God by claiming to. So, please read these next few pages as a guide only and pray about how you can implement these, and other ideas, into the lives of those around you.

Just as there is not one simple list of needs, or methods to solve them, neither is there a list of people who need help. Simply, your job is to help those with burdens. Who has burdens? Anyone and everyone. So, check your motive, your job, your responsibility, God's plan, and then let's help!

This is not a psychology textbook, a financial services guide or a childcare manual, this is a way of thinking and operating so that God's will is done through you.

In summarising this book so far, we see:
1. What do they need?
   Practical and eternal SALVATION

2. What is your role?
   Be available for God to work THROUGH

3. What enables you to help?
   The GIFT from God

4. What do you do?
   Be ready, able and willing to HELP

Help your enemies

Whether the help is saving someone from a rip, debt or sins, we *all* need rescuing from different situations at different times. One thing about being human is that problems grow. In this world, sin leads to more sin. Burdens lead to more burdens. And hurt leads to more hurt.

Jesus told a parable about the Good Samaritan in Luke chapter 10. Although we are now under grace and not law, the message is so important that he reinforced, in modern language, the requirement to help even those you do not love.

One of the many Laws of Justice and Mercy that God gave to Moses was: "If you see the donkey of someone who hates you fallen down under its load, do not leave it there; be sure you help him with it." (Exodus 23:5).

God had to be specific: *do not leave it there* and *be sure to help him with it*. We are not to be the judge and jury of those to whom God wants to show compassion and love. God is not telling us to help only those who are our friends or loved ones. He states clearly, "… of someone who hates you". In other words, help your enemies. Don't just be willing to help those whom you get on with; be just as willing (no, be more willing) to help those who don't like you. It will create a much better impression for the Kingdom.

We often get caught up in the church world of helping other Christians, which is great and please, don't stop. But they already know Jesus, they are already going to heaven. Please, share your generosity, your gifts, and your time with others who don't have that same advantage.

It may make it easier if you see that your *enemies* are not necessarily those who despise you. Just like *aliens* are not from another planet. We tend to slot people into boxes and the labels aren't always accurate. We tend to bracket people into the categories that we determine, based on our assumption that we are the correct race, character, age or whatever classification we refer to. By placing ourselves inside the bracket of perfection, we are saying that everyone outside of this, being not identical to us, is therefore less of a person than we are. Ironically, it also puts us outside the bracket of others so they're right to think the same thing of us.

God tells us to love our enemies and feed the aliens. He doesn't tell us to distinguish between them. Take a moment and think about how you categorise people into different groups. In your opinion, who is the 'perfect' person? Then, identify who your enemy really is.

So, when you are called to help someone, can you hold that baby if its skin is a different colour? Can you listen to the woman who is drunk again in her attempt at hiding the pain that her husband causes her every night? Can you give a lift to the person who has no money for fuel without judging how they prioritise their expenses?

Now, if everyone is loved by God, and we stop being judgemental, we need to look at those people who we generally lean towards helping, and those we tend to shy away from.

Imagine for a moment that a family with dirty clothes and unkempt hair attended your church or workplace. What would your reaction be? Would you want to offer them assistance, money, or a shower? Would you shoo them away because they 'don't fit' your environment? Or, would you embarrass them by treating them overtly special and ... different?

How do you know if they need, or even want, a shower or clean clothes? If their life has reached that stage, is cleanliness their greatest priority right now or could it perhaps be food or shelter? Or maybe the phone number of a lost relative? We tend to jump to conclusions, based on our own prejudices, when faced with what we perceive to be obvious needs.

Can you simply talk to them, as if they were equal to you, and get to know them? Can you take that conversation, in a respectful and non-judgemental manner to seek their real needs? Can you do this while you hand this person and this God-ordained interaction to God, asking for his input and guidance over this relationship?

I regret that I am unable to find the author to give them the credit, but I thank whoever wrote the following verse.

When we are given our rewards, I would prefer to have erred on the side of grace rather than judgement:

- To have loved too much rather than too little;
- To have forgiven the undeserving rather than refused forgiveness to that one who deserved it;
- To have fed a parasite rather than to have neglected one that was truly hungry;
- To have been taken advantage of rather than to have taken undue advantage;
- To have believed too much in my brothers rather than too little, having been wronged on the side of too much trust rather than too much cynicism;
- To have believed the best and been wrong, than to have believed the worst and been right.

The Full Imposition

Timothy chapter 5 talks about looking after widows. Verse 16 specifically tells us that if a widow (in need) has a family, they are to help her rather than the church helping her. In this way, the resources that the church has - time, accommodation, money, food - can be used to help those widows in need that don't have family to help. The verse reads, "If any woman who is a believer has widows in her family, she should help them and not let the church be burdened with them, so that the church can help those widows who are really in need."

It is interesting to note the word 'burdened' in this verse. We tend to think of that with negative connotations - a burden is something that holds us down, is pressed upon us, a duty or load. When the church takes on the responsibility for someone, as it has been given the responsibility for widows, it takes on the full imposition of helping them until the help is no longer needed. Likewise, when we help someone, we need to be willing to help them until it is no longer needed.

It is common for people to be surrounded by visitors immediately after a death or an operation, but what about when they are trying to return their life to normality, or when they go home. Don't forget about them after the immediate crisis. You may be able to assist them in gaining their independence or discovering a new ability. Many people don't discover what their partners did for them until they don't have them anymore. Often times, one couple pays the bills and takes care of the domestic duties. If that person is removed, the person left can find themselves unable to use the washing machine, use internet banking or know what song helps the toddler get to sleep. These are the times when people suffering need help, not just when they are surrounded by guests who let them cry.

In Matthew 11:28, Jesus told the crowd to, "Come to me, all you who are weary and burdened, and I will give you rest." Jesus was our example in this way. We are to assist those with burdens and allow them to rest. These burdens can be physical, spiritual, financial or emotional. What good is it carrying an able man's hat when a crippled woman is struggling with a heavy suitcase? What good is it to show directions on a map to a blind man? In the next three sections we will look practical, personal and spiritual help.

Key Points:
- There is no clear list of who to help and how, just be available;
- Sin leads to more sin, burdens lead to more burdens, hurt leads to more hurt;
- Help Christians & atheists, friends & enemies, neighbours & aliens;
- Identify differences, and be mindful not judgemental;
- Be willing to carry the load.

Practical Help

It is interesting to note the range of definitions given to the word "help" in the Macquarie Dictionary.

1. To do something with (a person) so that it is done more easily; aid, assist.
2. To give strength or means to contribute aid; assist in doing.
3. To relieve (someone) in need, sickness, pain or distress.
4. To be of use; remedy.
5. To contribute an improvement to.
6. To be of service or advantage.

When looking at ways to be helpful, a good starting point is to look at the basic human needs of shelter, food, water, and love. What is required to ensure that people have these basic essential items in their life? If we start with the big picture, the macro view of the world, we see that for people to have shelter, we need land. Therefore, caring for the environment is one way to assist in the provision of shelter for other people. You may like to use your resources in underprivileged areas or start recycling at home.

That was a very core place to start, but often we need to begin at the beginning, and get the foundations right to ensure that whatever else is placed on top of it will be sustained.

Too often, we can be *oh so spiritual* and talk about helping others get through their battles. We probably even pray for the person and their needs, but then we forget completely about the actual physical problem. Don't leave the load. As well as helping the person, see what practical assistance you can offer. That may be in the form of cooking a meal for the family whose mother is in hospital, driving someone to some event (maybe church), helping someone to move to a new house, helping a neighbour concrete their path or helping a child with their homework.

The Job Description in chapter 6 mentioned some practical examples of projects performed by previous employees: help with heavy loads; employ others to give them a financial start; provide food, drink, clothing, shelter; teach; lend or sell at no profit. I could make a list of "50 Ways to Help Others" but whatever number I chose the list would be too small. Why limit God when we can't.

In Psalm 10:14 we are instructed, "You are the helper of the fatherless." My first impression of this verse was to help the kids, but this verse means so much more. Helping the fatherless is practical advice because they'd be lacking things for sure. Again, wait on God's directions because these kids are lacking *a lot* and only God knows which void needs filling in which child in which way. Even a family of four children would each have different needs, priorities and values. Giving a casserole to four kids probably isn't going to help them call to The Father in a relationship. Taking those four to the movies is a nice idea, but it may bring about sad memories for one of them. The point is again, seek God's direction. After all, the goal is to lead them to God, so they can know, not just a father, but The Father.

Being realistic, fatherless children have less money, a very busy mum, lack of masculine help / authority / provision. There are a lot of needs. One point of advice, and another reason to seek God first: it is a sad state of our times that the household may actually be better off without the particular father that they had. The mother may be happy, very organised, and a good provider. Don't underestimate (or insult) her abilities by rushing in to provide what she may already have or has decided she does not need.

There *will* be needs - the Bible says so and that is our authority - just make sure you provide the needs God wants to provide for that family, not what you want to provide for that family. Women these days are very independent and capable. You may have identified a family without a father and want to help, good on you, that's the first step. However, coaching the mother into a closer relationship with God, where she can call on him for help and bring her to a place of dependence on him rather than on her own abilities, is much more beneficial (in this life and the next) than any amount of food you could cook her.

Ask yourself whether your help is a result of what you think they need, or what they think they need, or what God knows they need.

Practical help is not just giving them the resources

We need to get away from the way humans think. "Oh Lord my God, I called to you for help and you healed me." (Psalm 30:2).

It is not necessarily just physical, practical help that is needed. Don't be tempted to immediately give money. For some, paying all their bills just frees them to return to their habit or debt. Rather, teach them budgeting and menu planning. I'm not telling you this so you can take the easy way out. I'm telling you so you can be a part of doing a greater good. God doesn't just answer the prayer, he goes beyond.

One organisation uses this concept, the 40 Hour Famine. They don't just raise money to provide food. Their donations provide the tools for preparing the fields and the seeds for growing the crops that will feed the communities for years.

I recall my first Community College course, Basic Computers. I knew how to open it and type but wanted to know more of its functions. Most of the students had the same complaint: whenever we asked the teacher for help, she would take over our computers and do it for us at her expert speed. We learned nothing. She was of no help to us.

Leviticus 25:35 gives advice on helping in a practical way: "If one of your countrymen becomes poor and is unable to support himself among you, help him as you would an alien or a temporary resident, so he can continue to live among you."

Verse 36: "Do not take interest from him ... *but fear God.*"

Verse 37: "You *must not lend money to him at interest or sell him food at a profit.*"

Verse 38: "God gave you the land" (and provisions)

Verse 39: "Don't make him a slave"

Verse 40: "Treat him as a hired helper" - *give him paid work.*"

Sarah and I were talking about the need to know basic mechanics. We then discussed this as a great skill to teach other women who are learning to be independent, such as teenagers, widows, and single mums. As well as the mechanical skills, it would be good to teach women other tricks and tips to help them do what they haven't been able to, or haven't yet had the need to do.

Sarah is very petite, and she married a man who is extremely strong. Now separated, she is responsible for her car, but even though she knows how to change a tyre, she cannot physically undo the wheel nuts. My advice to her was to go to a tyre place and have them loosen the nuts to her strength (obviously still tight enough to be safe, but not to his excessive level), and to keep a can of WD40 in the car. These two tips were simple and inexpensive, but may prevent a single woman being stranded should she get a flat tyre.

Whatever the burden, sometimes people just need an extra set of hands. Not every problem needs *you* to go to God in prayer, often *you are the answer to the prayer*. Someone may have already prayed, and God has seen the need. You are the tool he is using to answer that need. Be prepared to be practical. So, if this call to action has occurred after you have given God permission to use you, you don't need to ask him, "How can I help?" It is better just to reaffirm that he is in control and thank him for the opportunity.

Helping is not always about providing practical help, sometimes it is about training the person to become more capable, but it is always about leading them to a closer relationship with God. Directly or indirectly, "In every way preach, where necessary, use words" (author unknown).

Key Points:
- Only God can see behind closed doors and into the hearts, lifestyles and bank balances of others;
- Be sure to provide the help God suggests, not what you think of;
- You may be the answer to prayer;
- Helping may involve preparing them to need less help;
- Helping is always leading them closer to God.

Personal Help

Just as we did with practical help, a good starting point is ensuring that others are receiving their basic emotional needs - a sense of purpose, self-worth, love, goals and acceptance. Meeting these personal needs may be as simple as the examples given in the Job Description in chapter 6: uplift someone after a fall or incident; visit the sick or imprisoned; encourage people; care for the sick; or tell someone they look good.

Complex requirements

Consider a garden. I am not much of a gardener, but I am relatively happy with what I've achieved, and my garden is as varied as my personality. In my garden I have ferns, succulents, annuals, perennials, herbs, vegetables, weeds, trees, shrubs and vines. I have succulents in teacups and in large pots. I have herbs in the ground and in pots. I have vines in the right place and in the wrong place.

I can't tell you the scientific name of any of these plants. (Mainly because I have no interest in learning long names I cannot remember or pronounce.) I cannot tell you how big any of them will grow or how long they will last. What I can tell you is the best position for them in every season, and how much water, sun and fertiliser they need.

You see, I spent a little time in the planning phase of my garden, but I observe my garden daily. I watch and act accordingly. As the seasons change, I know that Mr Fussy (our New Guinea Impatient) must be moved so he gets more, or less, direct sunlight.

I know that, by pinching the flowers off the Coleus, the nutrients go into making the leaves and stems strong, or they lose out in favour of temporary flowers. I know that if I don't use my Coriander, it will go to seed and die. I know that Sugar Herb really does taste sweet.

I have learned these things, not from textbooks, but because I enjoy my garden. I love my garden. I care for my garden. And I want the plants in my garden to have the best opportunity to be the best they can be and live without too much struggle.

I also know that struggles will come their way, and I know which ones will suffer the most. These ones get extra mulch, feed and water as the harshness of the summer heat and the winter frosts approach.

If you're not a gardener, I apologise for the analysis, but I liken us to plants in God's garden. Not only do we go through distinct, and ever changing, seasons. Not only does every person, and plant, react differently to the seasons they endure. Every season in our lives is tended to by a God who knows and cares for our every individual atom.

So, staying on the garden theme just a little longer, think of the water that each of my plants need. The succulent in the teacup needs about a quarter of a cup twice a week in Summer, once a week in Spring and Autumn, and once a fortnight in Winter.

Mr Fussy needs a 9-litre bucket daily in Summer. That's a big difference in the amount of water given to each. So, do I use my quarter cup of water for Mr Fussy? I could, but it would take a while. Do I pour my 9 litres of water on my teacup? I could, but it would flood out the succulent.

If you think this is complex, the help humans need constantly changes because our needs change with our everchanging circumstances. At least plants only have changes from season, time of day and soil conditions. The help humans need differs depending on the person, the current circumstances, the experiences that person has been through, the mental attitude, the spiritual strength, the physical strength, the obstacles…

Not all needs get help

We are told in 1 Timothy 5:11-15 that, if we do too much for people, they will become lazy. In those times, the church kept a register of the people they were to help. This passage specifically tells us *not* to put certain people on that list. God, knowing them so much better than we possibly could, has other ideas for them.

The verse says, "As for younger widows, do not put them on such a list. For when their sensual desires overcome their dedication to Christ, they want to marry. Thus, they bring judgment on themselves, because they have broken their first pledge. Besides, they get into the habit of being idle and going about from house to house. And not only do they become idlers but also gossips and busybodies, saying things they ought not to. So, I counsel younger widows to marry, to have children, to manage their homes and to give the enemy no opportunity for slander. Some have in fact already turned away to follow Satan."

Sometimes helping means saying no. We can look at Isaiah 30:7 for two very different interpretations of the same message. The KJV says: "For the Egyptians shall help in vain, and to no purpose: therefore, have I cried concerning this, their strength is to sit still." The NIV interprets this as: "To Egypt, whose help is utterly useless. Therefore, I call her Rahab the Do-Nothing." Either way, the actions that the Egyptians did was of no use at all.

Sadly, this is what I did for all those years; I helped in vain, to no purpose. My help was utterly useless. I might as well have done nothing. When I received the prophecy to say that I was to be a helper, I became very busy. I knew that God was teaching me new things, but the idea of me staying back and washing up after church supper, well that was a new concept. I've always hated housework, so why would I help wash up at church? Because it was helping. So, I thought that God had done well by making me into the helper he wanted me to be. I was always helping other people.

Now, please, do not stop providing the help that you are, at least not until you have spent many hours meditating and talking to God about this to find out what he wants you to do. It may be that your place is to help with the washing up. For a time, that may even have been my place. The point is, don't *you* make the decision as to what helping is and what you should be doing with your every day. Let God make those decisions for you.

Practical help is not always the best method. Sometimes, we need to be there to ride the storm with someone. We just need to be there alongside them. Attend court with them. Go shopping with them. Sit and listen to them talk or cry. Be there.

However, please stay alert and, even while doing personal tasks, don't get personally involved. One job I had was to help a business get their financial and administrative affairs in order. I was only meant to help for a few weeks but six months later I was still there. I became personally involved.

When you have accepted the job of God's helper, you need to keep a certain distance from those you help. Some call this wearing a mask, but it is for their good as well as yours. It also keeps your family and friends in the special place they deserve to be, closer to you than anyone else.

Once we become personally involved, we let the other parties see inside us, and let them see our flaws. By keeping a professional distance, they see the help that occurs and the miracle of God's love in that event. When they see us, the focus changes and the true purpose of our presence is detracted as our personalities get in the way.

Don't overstay your visit or your welcome. After all, you usually don't need the person to get to know you, you need them to get to know God. Show them God, then move on.

Remember that it is not always wise to do the job for the person; often it is more beneficial to assist them to do the task. This way, not only do you relieve some of the burden from them, making the task more manageable, but they get to see the life of Jesus alive on earth. You also giving them the necessary skills to prevent the same thing happening again. And, who knows, one day they may help someone else faced with the same problem.

This type of assistance contrasts with the person who would not forgive. When one is forgiven, they are meant to learn forgiveness from that and show forgiveness to others. Likewise, when one is helped by being taught something, they are then in a position to share that with someone else in need.

Key Points:

- Live in his will so your spiritual ears (senses) are open;
- Every person is complex, and requirements will vary person to person, day to day...Like a garden, people have different requirements in different seasons of life;
- Sometimes helping means saying no;
- Sometimes we need to ride the storm with them;
- Helping people learn the skills to get out of their dilemma enables them to help another in the same situation.

Spiritual Help

As well as practical and personal help, there is also spiritual help. This involves tasks like helping others to live in God's will; performing miracles; praying for workers; praying for those in need; and strengthening other peoples' faith. In Psalm 34:17-18, "The righteous cry out, and the Lord hears them; he delivers them from all their troubles. The Lord is close to the brokenhearted and saves those who are crushed in spirit."

Spiritual help is just that, spiritual help. It is using your access to God's resources to help another person become a greater God resource. It is not a 'holier-than-thou' ego opportunity, nor is it a magical, mystical fantasy. Spirituality for God's people is the part of our being that is in relation with the God who created us. Part of it is helping in the world with resources that are seen and acknowledged in the human sphere - including emotional and mental support - providing the right resources to the right person at the right time.

Over and above this assistance is spiritual aide. Praying with someone, teaching, helping and encouraging others to pray. Going with them as they approach the pastor or God. Sharing Bible passages with them.

Sometimes, it means helping them to see that God wants us to learn from our experiences. Bad circumstances don't make us bad people. They don't mean that we failed, and they certainly don't mean that we are worth less than anyone else in God's eyes.

In fact, bad experiences are in our lives for a reason. They test us and make us stronger. They give us opportunities to gain valuable insight, which allows us to help other people through similar circumstances. Have you ever wondered why the Ten Plagues happened? Were they God's revenge for a situation he didn't see coming? Never! Were they God's unjust and irrational anger at play? Never! The Ten Plagues were sent so that Pharaoh, the other gods, and the people would all see God's power and turn to him to receive his love.

We need to trust that God knows the bigger picture so don't limit God's input by structuring your prayer requests too specifically. If someone you love is going out to celebrate their birthday, it may not be wise to ask God to, "ensure they have fun". Their idea of having fun may be getting drunk. Being drunk may lead to them getting raped or beaten. Your specific request may not be in their best interests. Besides, God never once instructed us to ask for fun. Instead, trust God that he knows what's best and ask him to be with them and protect them.

Healing is *not* related to how spiritual a person is. If God can use your situation, let him. Jean was on dialysis for years before her transplant. As if that wasn't enough to endure, many church people told her, "If you would pray better", or "You're obviously not walking in God's will". She was doing everything right, including witnessing to nursing staff - an opportunity to reach people that the well-meaning Christians didn't have.

I recall a story that had a great impact on me. A man, being told of yet another blow to his life, a new insurmountable illness, responded with an attitude that I can only aspire to. He didn't say, "Why me, poor me." Instead, his response was, "Well, why not me?"

The cycle shows us that the starting point is not always the same. We can enter the cycle anywhere, depending on our spiritual understanding and relationship with God at that moment in time. Wherever the person in need is at, the helper's motive must remain the same: to bless man and glorify God.

Mark 9:24 shows a father who brought a possessed son to Jesus and asked, "If you can do anything, take pity and help." Then, when Jesus questioned him, he exclaimed, "I do believe, help me overcome by unbelief." God knew that the condition of this man's son was a tool to bring this father to the realisation that his faith needed work. Jesus knew exactly the right actions and words to have this man seek a closer relationship with God. God didn't cause this boy to be possessed, but he certainly knew about it, and took the opportunity to bring a child of his own closer by asking for help.

Jesus spoke to the crowd, both Christians and non-Christians alike. Therefore, to be like him, we have an obligation to help both Christians and non-Christians. After many years, I re-read my prophecy and discovered it was a much bigger task than I had realised. The prophecy for me was that I'd help in the church. This is probably why I so easily took to washing up, my initial understanding of the church was the institution. I hadn't yet learned that God's church is his people. After helping in several churches, I still cannot think of a better training ground.

Jesus commanded us to go and preach, so I don't believe we are restricted to helping in church. We can't put God in a box, and this is his ministry. So, I urge you to help outside of church too. Help non-Christians also.

"So do not fear; for I am with you, do not be dismayed, for I am your God. I will strengthen you and help you; I will uphold you with my righteous right hand." (Isaiah 41:10).

Sometimes, we ignore his instructions or get it wrong, so he uses another method or tool to help. I recall one time where I firmly believed that he told me to cross the road and talk to a particular person. Feeling shy, I ignored it and then felt guilty for a long time. He reminded me that he will have his way, he would use another person or another experience to reach that person. In that case, I was the one missing out on the opportunity to work with God on a project that brings another to salvation. God always has his way and the person in need gets help. I am the one who misses out on using the gift God gave me.

Key Points:

- Bad experiences are in our lives for a reason;
- The motive is always to bless man and glorify God;
- We are not restricted to help either believers or non-believers. Help both;
- Helping in an environment where others have similar skills is a good training ground;
- If I miss an opportunity to help God, he will use another. I miss out.

Application for Chapter 11: The Needees' Needs

1. Think of 5 people close to you. What needs do they currently have? Select one and write it down.

   _____
   _____
   _____
   _____

2. Now think of 5 people that you don't really know well, possibly a sales assistant. What needs could they currently have? Select one and write it down.

   _____
   _____
   _____
   _____

3. Think of a time when you felt distant from God. How did you feel? How was your life? What could have helped bring you closer to him?

   _____
   _____
   _____

4. What did you learn from the previous experience that could help another person in the same situation?

_____

_____

5. Select one Bible reference mentioned in this chapter. Write it out on another piece of paper and put it on your fridge. Memorise it this week. What does this verse mean to you personally?

_____

_____

6. Identify one local need that you have a passion for. What can you do to help? Make a plan.

_____

_____

_____

7. Pray about the needs you identified in the first two questions, asking God if these are needs that he wants your involvement in and what he wants you to do to help them. Ask him for opportunities to be the tool in his hands that he uses to help these people.

Salvation through the gift of HELP…

Chapter 12: Bless Man & Glorify God

Helping others leads to their salvation as it deepens yours. The goal, purpose, motive and passion should always be to bless man and glorify God.

Helping in the right way

Sometimes, we can get caught up in thinking rather than doing. We can spend a lot of time assessing, analysing and planning - how can I help? But the gift of help is not about your plans, it is about being available as God needs you to be. This means being available (not too busy), alert and attentive, and aware of your surroundings.

I'm sure you know that not all opportunities to help are listed in a directory or a diary, but sometimes God makes the instructions very clear. In Deuteronomy 22:1-4 we are specifically told: "If you see your brother's ox or sheep straying, do not ignore it but be sure to take it back to him. If the brother does not live near you or if you do not know who he is, take it home with you and keep it until he comes looking for it. Then give it back to him. Do the same if you find your brother's donkey or his cloak or anything he loses. Do not ignore it. If you see your brother's donkey or his ox fallen on the road, do not ignore it. Help him get it to his feet." While some people may have the opportunity to take these literally, we usually need to be flexible in our understanding and relate them to situations that occur in our own lives.

Of course, Jesus expounds on this moral in a parable about the Good Samaritan. In that story, a man was robbed and beaten and then left for dead. Sadly, both a priest and a Levite passed by and ignored the victim. Both should have known what to do, both were fully trained in the religious duties of the day and both knew the Bible.

However, it was a Samaritan that helped the man. Taking time out of his day, he took pity on him, bandaged him, poured oil on him, took him to an inn and paid for his treatment.

Now this example wasn't just told to show how we are to be nice to others. It was Jesus' answer to questions about how to inherit eternal life. He was explaining how to love God with all your heart, soul, strength and mind.

Every Christian believes in God and we all need help with our faith at times. As helpers, you and I are called to help with this aspect of their lives as well. When confronted with this I cried to the Lord, "God, how can I help strengthen other people's faith?"

Do I strengthen their faith when I help them build their fence? Yes, when you do it right. Do I strengthen their faith when I give them money? Yes, when you do it right. Do I strengthen their faith when I pray for their healing? Yes, when you do it right. Do I strengthen their faith when I visit them in hospital? Yes, when you do it right.

So, how do I do it right? How do I help others in the right way? We learned that helping can be done in the wrong way, but how do we help in the right way? By ensuring that God makes the decisions, not you. By being guided by God as to who to help, how and when.

I assume you know the message in the Bible about, "some plant seeds, some water, some reap the fruit". Only God knows every person's walk. Only God knows the true level of each person's faith. Only God knows where your help fits into the path of their salvation. Your job is to be obedient and act as he calls. Let the working out be done by him.

So, if he calls you to speak to someone about the gospel, speak. It doesn't have to be at church, it doesn't have to involve a formal invitation to discuss such affairs. It may be as simple as saying out loud, "Praise God for the quality of this timber," while you are helping a neighbour build a fence.

You may be the answer to a heart's call for a sign from God. I've heard many stories where a person has heard about God, but challenged him with, "God, if you are real, then send someone to take me to church / help with the phone bill / provide me with food ..." The list is endless, and we cannot possibly know about those calls until *after* salvation and only *if* that person testifies of it. How many people call out to God for a sign and they don't get it because we, his chosen workers, choose not to help in that way or aren't available on that day? How many souls don't go to heaven because we didn't play our part? You *must* be available when God calls, and you *must* live a life close enough to God, so you hear him when he does call you.

Key Points:
- Be available, alert, attentive and aware;
- Your job is to be obedient; he will work out the details;
- Take all opportunities to praise God;
- You may be the answer to a heart's call for a sign from God;
- Could you bear knowing a soul didn't go to heaven because you didn't play your part?

Cleanse Your Life

Your character becomes your destiny. Your character can enrich your life on earth with a deep relationship with God; a relationship that leads to eternity in heaven. By saving others from the situation they are in, you are helping them to also live a life on earth rich in the relationship with God that leads to eternity in heaven for them.

Luke 6:45 says, "The good man brings good things out of the good stored up in his heart, and the evil man brings evil things out of the evil stored up in his heart. For out of the overflow of his heart his mouth speaks."

Gossip

One of the lies of the modern-day church is 'sharing in love' where one member shares the private details of another. "I am only telling you this because I'm worried about this person I love, and I know you'll pray for them..." Stop. It's gossip! It's wrong! Do you, in the deepest parts of your heart and mind, honestly believe that you are helping the person you're talking about?

If you have faith that God can help them, then you don't need your friend to pray for them. You pray for them. The only thing you are doing by sharing the knowledge you have is influencing the negative thought pattern of another person towards a third party. Stop gossiping.

Do it with a smile

Whatever your role is in helping another, whether your part is big or small, do it with a smile. Even if your role is to walk away doing nothing, or simply leaving them with a few words, the one thing they will see is your smile. Helen Steiner Rice wrote a beautiful poem called Smile:

> *When you do what you do with a will and a smile*
> *Everything that you do will seem twice as worthwhile*
> *And when you walk down the street, life will seem twice as sweet*
> *If you smile at the people you happen to meet.*
> *For when you smile it is true folks will smile back at you.*
> *So do what you do with a will and a smile*
> *And whatever you do will be twice as worthwhile.*

Paul, in his tireless work spreading the gospel, said in Colossians 1:29 that, "To this end I labour, struggling with all his energy, which so powerfully works in me."

I firmly believe the following saying to be true of just about everything: The more you get the more you want, and the less you get the less you want. Think about it. The more sleep you get, the more sleep you want and vice versa. The more food you get, the more you want, and the less you get, your stomach seems to shrink, and you crave less. I think this applies to sex, alcohol, sugar, drugs, money, work, exercise, health, beauty, fashion, Bible knowledge ... everything.

So, it is wise to want more of what God wants in your life and remove those things that he doesn't want for you. You can change. 1 Corinthians 2:9b-10 encourages us with, "No eye has seen, no ear has heard, no mind has conceived what God has prepared for those who love him - but God has revealed it to us by his Spirit."

When I realised this, I made a new goal - to cleanse my life.

Not in any order, this is how my brainstorming list started:

I want more of…	I want less of…
Writing	Back pain
God's influence	Meetings
Quality family time	Expenses

Start enjoying the journey as you work towards the plans God has for you. Psalm 40:5 reminds us that, "Many, O Lord my God, are the wonders you have done. The things you planned for us no one can recount to you; were I to speak and tell of them, they would be too many to declare."

So, what will *your* next phase look like? Proverbs 19:21 tells us, 'Many are the plans in a man's heart, but it is the Lord's purpose that prevails.' Kneel before God and tell him what your ideas and interests are, and ask him to show you part of his purpose for you.

The Challenge of Outreach, author unknown

> *Go:*
>> *Out from the warmth and joy of fellowship in your church*
>> *Out because Christ commanded us to go*
>> *Out because we, as Christians, are His ambassadors*
>> *Out in obedience because we love Christ*
>> *Out because we care for the lost*
>> *Out to those who do not know Christ as saviour*
>
> *Into the highways and hedges:*
>> *Where a baby is born every two seconds*
>> *Where parental and juvenile delinquency are rampant*
>> *Where life's highways lead to school, office, shop or store*
>> *Where people are groping for meaning in life*

That:
The seeker may find truth
The sorrowing may find comfort
The weary may find rest
The troubled may find peace
The sinner may find eternal life.

Key Points:
- Check your motivation and the methods will produce fruit;
- Stop gossiping;
- The more you want, the more you get. The less you want, the less you get;
- You can change;
- Start working towards the plans God has for you.

Bless Man and Glorify God

Salvation is both the first step and the result. Throughout this book, you have read this phrase a lot: bless man and glorify God. This saying is my simplified summary of what should be our motivation in everything we do.

I assume that you know the story of David and Goliath, the small boy who killed the giant. For a refresher, read 1 Samuel 17:25-26. David had the right attitude. When faced with the giant, others thought only two things: he is too big for us to defeat, and what will the winner gain.

David's attitude was to bless man and glorify God. He wanted to remove this disgrace from Israel, "who does he think he is". And he had no doubt that God was the one in control, adamant that God deserved the victory.

When I become aware of someone who is ill or injured, I pray. God, unless you have a reason for *not* healing them, please heal them. And please bless all those involved - medical personnel, family, spectators and others. God is the author of multitasking. In any one event, he changes more than just the recipient. In a simple act of goodness, God changes the doer, the one in need, and the onlookers.

I was putting air in the last tyre as a well-dressed lady pulled up beside me. Window down, we spoke briefly about local air pumps. I offered to do her tyres for her, "I'm out of the car and dirty already. It's silly us both getting out." And I proceeded to inflate her tyres.

I finished and said, "You're done for another month".

"Thank you very much. Can I buy you a coffee or something for it?"

I replied, "No, but what a lovely gesture, thank you." Then added, "You can do one thing for me. You can pray."

She simply answered, "Okay" and I was on my way.

Now I could have left it there, but it didn't feel complete so, as I was driving, I prayed.

"God, I claim salvation through the gift of help. I helped. I planted a seed, a link to you. Now the rest is up to you."

He quickly and lovingly replied, "It always is".

Yes, salvation is dependent on him. I will probably never see this woman again, and there is no more I can do. She is in God's hands, with the memory of a little helper and a seed requesting her to pray. Little things in her mind for God to come into her heart and save her.

Glorifying God isn't the same as saying thanks to him silently after he has helped us with something. Giving him the glory also means acknowledging his input publicly. It means giving him the credit instead of taking it for ourselves. It also means living in a way that represents him, not bringing shame to him. It means loving his people the way he does, and that involves helping them.

Psalm 69:5-6 is a strong reminder to be a good example to others so that they will turn *to* God rather than *away* from him. As David reveals, we won't always get it right, but try. "You know my folly, O God; my guilt is not hidden from you. May those who hope in you not be disgraced because of me, O Lord, the Lord Almighty; may those who seek you not be put to shame because of me, O God of Israel."

For a long time, I thought this phrase was the wrong way around. Surely, our priority should be first to glorify God, and then to bless people. One morning God helped me to see that it is correct.

We don't just go out into our day and glorify God without doing anything. Standing on a sidewalk breathing in and out doesn't bring him much attention. It's in our service to others, our helping others, that we have the opportunities to bring him the that glory he deserves. It's in the way we act, the way we speak, to whom we choose to give the credit. It's *by* blessing others that God gets the glory! Besides, tongue in cheek, it sounds better this way.

When God is in it, everyone wins. I think David summed it up perfectly in Psalm 70:4b when he said, "May those who love your salvation always say, 'Let God be exalted!'"

If we truly understand that our salvation is dependent on Jesus' death on the cross, and we honestly appreciate that we are going to spend eternity in heaven, then we must wholly believe that we are children of God. If this is the case, then we should value others as children of God too, and therefore want them to experience the joy of that salvation. Then, we show our love of salvation by giving the praise to God, both for his glory and so that others hear it and, in turn, do the same.

Hence, Bless Man and Glorify God.

Key Points:

- Have David's attitude: God is in control and he deserves the victory;
- When helping others, help them link it back to God;
- In one act of goodness. God changes the doer, the one in need, and the onlookers.
- It's by blessing others that God gets the glory;
- Glorifying God means living in a way that represents him, not bringing shame to him;

May Paul write about you

When Paul wrote to the Philippians, he wrote with joy and wisdom. He knew they were a people striving to please God, doing God's work. And because of this, Paul could give them further instruction as to how to do that better, and how to be even closer to the God they all loved and served. I hope that you may experience someone writing a letter about you, but if not, know that your details are already in heaven with God.

In the first chapter of Philippians, Paul writes, "I thank my God every time I remember you ... because of your partnership in the gospel … being confident of this, that he who began a good work in you will carry it on to completion until the day of Jesus Christ."

He goes on to say, "And this is my prayer: that your *love* may abound more and more in *knowledge* and *depth of insight*, so that you may be *able to discern* what is best … filled with the *fruit of righteousness* that comes *through Jesus Christ - to the glory and praise of God.*"

I pray that you go on to help others with the needs God has in store for them; that you be a tool that God can use whenever and however he wants; that your life be fulfilled as you continue to *bless man and glorify God.*

Key Points:
- Make your life one that people want to record;
- Is your life on earth worthy of response?
- What will be written in your obituary;
- God has a record in heaven of your life here on earth;
- When putting pen to paper or word to mouth, remember that all these assets belong to God.

Application for Chapter 12:
Bless Man & Glorify God

1. What could you do to cleanse your life? Start your list

   I want MORE of ...

   _____

   _____

   I want LESS of ...

   _____

   _____

2. What role is your salvation playing in the lives of others?

   _____

   _____

3. How is God working through you?

   _____

   _____

4. What has God given you that you can use to help other people?

   _____

   _____

5. Select one Bible reference mentioned in this chapter. Write it out on another piece of paper and put it on your fridge. Memorise it this week. How can this verse change your way of seeing your relationship with God?

_____
_____
_____

6. What 3 steps can you take to make yourself more available to God when he calls you to help someone?

_____
_____
_____

7. Pray that you can be a tool in God's hand to do his works here on earth. Pray that you can be the shell that he works through so that everything you do will bless man and glorify God. Feel free to make any notes here that resulted from that prayer time.

_____
_____
_____

References:

Anderson, Neil T. Renewing Your Mind. Bethany House Publishers, 2014.

Gwynn, Mark and Amanda Laugesen (ed). Australian Concise Oxford Dictionary. (6th edn). Oxford University Press, 2017.

Mason, Mearle. "Take Me." n.d.

Meece, David. "Things You Never Gave Me." There I Go Again. Aluminium Records, 2002. CD.

Meece, David. "We Are the Reason." Odyssey. By David Meece. Star Song, 1995. Compact Disc.

Pay It Forward. By Leslie Dixon. Dir. Mimi Leder. Prod. Peter Abrams. Warner Bros., 2000.

Raynor, Jordan. Called to Create. Baker Books. 2017.

Rice, Helen Steiner. Put your problems in God's hands. n.d.

Roebert, Pastor Andrew. "Alive to God." Thought for Today. Prod. Pastor Andrew Roebert. Glenstantia, 2018.

Strong, James. Strong's Exhaustive Concordance. Abingdon Press.1890

Truthbook. "The Drowning Man". Ed. The Urantia Book n.d. Truthbook. 7 February 2020. <https://truthbook.com/stories/funny-god/the-drowning-man>.

Walsh, Sheila. Loved Back to Life. Nashville: Nelson Books, 2015

Worldometer https://www.worldometers.info/demographics/life-expectancy 19 March 2020

Yates. Yates Garden Guide. 44th ed., Harper Collins, Australia. 2015

YouVersion. YouVersion Bible App. Edmond: Life Church, 2019. <http://youversion.com

Thank you all

www.ingramcontent.com/pod-product-compliance
Lightning Source LLC
Chambersburg PA
CBHW050626300426
44112CB00012B/1684